I0468429

Happiness

4 Simple Steps to Be Happy Here & Now - All You Need is Within You Now

Sam Hanson

Contents

© Copyright 2015 by Walter Spivak
- All rights reserved.

This document is geared towards providing exact and reliable information in regards to the topic and issue covered. The publication is sold with the idea that the publisher is not required to render accounting, officially permitted, or otherwise, qualified services. If advice is necessary, legal or professional, a practiced individual in the profession should be ordered.

- From a Declaration of Principles which was accepted and approved equally by a Committee of the American Bar Association and a Committee of Publishers and Associations.

In no way is it legal to reproduce, duplicate, or transmit any part of this document in either electronic means or in printed format. Recording of this publication is strictly prohibited and any storage of this document is not allowed unless with written permission from the publisher. All rights reserved.

The information provided herein is stated to be truthful and consistent, in that any liability, in terms of inattention or otherwise, by any usage or abuse of any policies, processes, or directions contained within is the solitary and utter responsibility of the recipient reader. Under no circumstances will any legal responsibility or blame be held against the publisher for any reparation, damages, or monetary loss due to the information herein, either directly or indirectly.

Respective authors own all copyrights not held by the publisher.

The information herein is offered for informational purposes solely, and is universal as so. The presentation of the information is without contract or any type of guarantee assurance.

The trademarks that are used are without any consent, and the publication of the trademark is without permission or backing by the trademark owner. All trademarks and brands within this book are for clarifying purposes only and are the owned by the owners themselves, not affiliated with this document.

Introduction

Everyone has days when they don't feel great and are lacking in energy. It is easy just to sit back and let the blues overwhelm you while you feel sorry for yourself. Then, the next day, when you are, hopefully, feeling better, you suddenly realize just how much time you wasted by allowing yourself to feel down. If only you could find ways of changing your state of mind from a negative one to a more positive one. The good news is that there are different ways that you can change your state of mind – and, with a bit of practice, in just a few minutes.

This book provides advice for people who are in a negative state of mind and want to get out of it as soon as possible. Of course, it will take more than a minute to digest the information contained in these pages and to get to the point where you are ready to put it into practice, but once you have, you should literally be able to change your state of mind within a minute.

The chapters in this book contain advice on the following strategies to change your state of mind:

- Cognitive behavioral therapy

- Meditation

- Exercise

- Visualization

In some cases, you may want to seek the advice of an expert in order to hone your skills before you are ready to follow them through at home; in other cases, you may find the tips in this book enough to set you on your way to a more positive state of mind. Of course, you may find one method more natural than another; in which case, that is probably the best one to undertake.

Of course, this book comes with the caveat that, if you are truly depressed and are struggling to see the point of life, the tips here are unlikely to make you feel much better about yourself and you should see a doctor for medical advice. Clinical depression needs long-term therapy and probably medication too. However, for those days when you are just feeling more cynical than usual, the tips in the following chapters should be of help. Certainly, many people have found these methods useful.

Thanks again for downloading this book, I hope you enjoy it!

Chapter 1:
Cognitive Behavioral Therapy

Cognitive behavioral therapy (CBT) is a type of therapy usually linked with depression and other mental health-related conditions. However, the basic premise, that it challenges the links between thoughts, feelings and behaviors, is just as useful for those who are feeling a bit down and need something to help them get back on track. This chapter will introduce cognitive behavioral therapy and will discuss how it can eventually be used at home to change your state of mind in just a minute.

What is cognitive behavioral therapy?

Whereas other types of psychotherapy can last for months or even years, cognitive behavioral therapy is usually short-term. If you decide to opt for sessions with a therapist, you can expect to be asked to attend for anything from six to twenty sessions. It is usually conducted on a one-on-one basis with a therapist, but in some cases, family members or friends may be asked to attend too.

The sessions will usually be very structured, unlike other forms of talking therapies, and aim to challenge negative feelings and behaviors. As the Mayo Clinic explains, the sessions will usually follow four steps:

- You will identify what is upsetting you

- You will share your feelings, thoughts and fears about what is upsetting you

- You will identify what is untrue or inaccurate about your feelings

- You will challenge what is false or inaccurate about your feelings

So, for example, you may identify that it is a row with your partner that is upsetting you and you may state that the row has made you feel insecure, unloved and possibly threatened. However, once you identify that feeling insecure and unloved is untrue because you know your partner really loves you and wants to make things work just as much as you do, then you can start to challenge those feelings and hopefully leave the session feeling more positive about making things up with your partner.

Initially, it may be very difficult for you to face up to what is bothering you and admit it out loud, let alone start sifting through your emotions and challenging them. However, you will find it easier with practice. Your therapist will usually give you homework so that you put the skills you have learned into use in between sessions. This way, you can put the skills that you have learned into practice straight away and build on your awareness of your feelings.

Could cognitive behavioral therapy help you?

Turning to therapy may not appeal to you at first, and you may hate the idea of being referred to a therapist for one-on-one sessions. It may not be necessary. Cognitive behavioral therapy is considered useful if you have depression, anxiety, anger management issues, marital problems, eating problems, personality issues or some other form of mental health problem. However, the way that problems are identified and then challenged could be of use to you in your everyday life.

If you have the time, and especially if you have problems that you don't think you can overcome by positive thinking, then it is definitely advisable to seek the advice of your doctor, who can then refer you to a therapist. There are strategies that you can take away from cognitive behavioral therapy to use at home in your own time. It may take you much longer than a minute to change your state of mind at first, but with practice, you should be able to recognize issues and challenge them quickly and easily.

Steps to follow at home

There are many different websites that offer to take you through the steps of cognitive behavioral therapy at home, and these may be of use to you. However, what they boil down to is (1) identifying the problem or situation, (2) identifying how it is making you feel, (3) deciding what is inaccurate or untrue about how you are feeling and then (4) challenging your feelings.

On a piece of paper, draw a table with four columns for each step. Then identify the problem, such as a concern that you have upset a colleague, and think about how it is making you feel – perhaps you feel guilty and uncomfortable, for example. Try to take a mental step back for a second and think about the issue from a bystander's point of view. Would a bystander think you should feel guilty and uncomfortable? Probably not. The next step is to challenge and rationalize how you are feeling; perhaps, for example, your colleague is having a bad time and would have reacted badly to anything, or maybe you were being human and made a mistake.

The process may seem cumbersome at first, but it does get easier with practice, and it will make you feel better. For the first few times that you practice it, write everything down; it may well be useful to look back at past sessions to see how you have improved. In time, you will probably find yourself applying the skills you've used without even noticing and will be able to do it in your head rather than having to write it all down. Once you have reached that stage, you should be able to improve the way that you are thinking in just a minute.

You don't need to have a form of mental illness in order to practice cognitive-behavioral therapy. You can use the strategies upon which cognitive behavioral therapy hinges in your own life to help you manage stressful and upsetting life situations more efficiently. It will involve a lot of practice before you can use it to challenge your state of mind in just a minute, but once you have reached that point, you will have an excellent way of challenging any negative thoughts that crop up during the course of your life.

Chapter 2:
Meditation

According to the Buddhist Center, meditation is a way of transforming the mind. For some people, the idea of sitting alone and trying to clear the mind of all that is going on may seem like an impossible feat. However, by practicing meditation on a regular basis, it can be very calming and, in time, can be an invaluable and time-efficient stress management tool.

Types of meditation

There are many types of meditation. You may choose to go to classes to help yourself 'get into the zone' in the first place, although you can easily meditate at home. In such classes, the teacher will guide you through a number of steps aimed at clearing your mind of unnecessary thoughts. This could include visualization, which will be discussed in more depth in chapter 4.

Other types of meditation involve chanting a mantra, either out loud or silently; mindfulness meditation, which involves focusing on the present moment and casting out the past; and transcendental meditation, which involves silently chanting a mantra that has been chosen for you personally. Sometimes meditation can be linked to exercise, such as yoga or tai chi. In all cases, you will need to concentrate on your breathing – and, if you take classes, you will be taught different ways of breathing in order to focus your thoughts on something other than what is bothering you.

It can certainly be useful to take classes if you have never practiced meditation before, just so that you understand what you need to do; for example, the breathing techniques mentioned above and how best to make yourself comfortable so that you can reap all the benefits of meditation. However, there are many self-help tutorials available online so that you can practice at home if you prefer.

Benefits of meditation

There are believed to be both physical and mental benefits to meditation. On a physical level, experts have found that practicing meditation on a regular basis can lower blood pressure, decrease pain, increase the amount of serotonin in the body, improve the immune system and increase your energy levels as your negative thoughts are channeled into a more positive way of thinking. On a mental level, you can gain greater peace of mind and thereby reduce stress and anxiety levels. With time and practice, your emotional health should improve too, as you learn more about yourself and how your mind works. The aim is that you let go of what is upsetting you and learn to live in the moment, thereby putting the past where it belongs – in the past.

How to meditate at home

By following a few simple tips, you can easily meditate at home, or even at work, provided that you can find somewhere quiet and peaceful. It may take practice before you can reap the benefits of just one minute meditation, but once you have reached that point, you will never look back.

To meditate in the traditional sense, you will ideally need to find somewhere quiet where you are unlikely to be disturbed.

This could be your bedroom, but wherever you are comfortable is fine; you could even try meditating outdoors if you prefer. Sit in a cross-legged position on the floor, or lie down, whatever you find most comfortable. There is no need for background music unless you find that it helps you.

Start by taking some deep breaths and try to relax every part of your body. Concentrate on the parts of your body that feel tense and try to let the stress ooze out of your muscles. If it helps, travel around your body in your mind and think about the sensations you are feeling in each part of you. Continue deep breathing while you are doing so.

It may help you to repeat the mantra, particularly if you find that your mind is always wandering. This could be something that you have picked up from meditation classes or found online, or it could simply be a word or phrase that you like, provided that it is not linked to something that you are trying to deal with.

To begin with, you may find that you can't meditate for more than a few minutes at a time; that is fine, just bear with it. Once you are well-practiced at meditation, you should be able to use your skills to de-stress whenever necessary, spending just a minute or two a day to change your state of mind.

If sitting still and concentrating on your breathing is something that you struggle with, you could try walking and meditating. Find a place to walk where you are unlikely to be disturbed and concentrate on the way that your muscles are working as you move. This will primarily be your legs and feet, but your arms, shoulders and torso also have a role. Think about the fresh air that you are breathing into your lungs and take deep breaths as you are doing so.

Many people meditate without even realizing. If you are religious, prayer could be your way of meditating, or you may be able to switch off unwanted thoughts while you are exercising. Experiment with what suits you best and, when you have found it, use it in your everyday life to deal with situations that are causing your anxiety. Before long, you will be able to meditate for short bursts, maybe just a minute at a time, thereby changing your negative thoughts into more positive ones and re-charging your batteries at the same time.

Chapter 3:
Exercise

Exercise is an excellent way of making yourself feel better. Unfortunately, few of us take advantage of the many benefits that exercise provides, especially when it is hard enough to fit work and home life into a daily routine. However, it really is worth finding the time to fit exercise into your daily routine, both from a physical and mental point of view.

How exercise can change your state of mind

Much research has been done into the link between exercise and feeling good. Experts have found that, when exercising, chemicals called endorphins are released into your body. These chemicals then interact with brain receptors, which reduces the body's perception of pain and makes you feel better in general. Many sportspeople talk about the sense of euphoria that they feel after exercising; this is caused by the release of endorphins into the body.

There are, of course, further benefits to exercising on a regular basis. As your body reacts to the exercise, you will lose weight, lower your blood pressure, your skin will become clearer; you will sleep better, and you will feel more energized. You'll probably also be encouraged to eat more healthily. All of this combined will make you feel better about yourself, which is why doctors often suggest that those suffering from depression, anxiety and other mental illnesses try to fit some exercise into their lives.

You don't, however, need to turn into a sportsperson to reap the benefits of feeling better through exercise. Just by fitting in a few minutes of exercise a day, you can cut down on your negative energy and increase your positive energy, thereby changing your state of mind.

If you hate exercise, you may not be aware of just how good it can make you feel, so you should give it a try. If you are very unfit or have a medical condition, you may want to check with your doctor before starting an exercise program; however, most doctors will agree that fitting some exercise into your life will be a positive step. Just don't try too much too soon; if you haven't walked further than to the end of your road in years, then don't be tempted to go for a jog until you feel that you are able to.

Types of exercise to make you feel good

The kind of exercise that you choose is really up to you because any form of exercise should help to make you feel better. If you're not really an exercising sort of person, it's worth experimenting with different types to find something that you like doing, because if you don't like your chosen type of exercise, you are unlikely to want to do it, especially when you're in a negative frame of mind.

Walking is something that virtually everyone can do. When you're feeling down, just getting outside into the fresh air and putting one foot in front of the other can really help put things into perspective. If you concentrate on how your muscles are working, you can fit in meditation as well.

Yoga is another excellent way of calming yourself down. It also has the advantage that you can exercise the whole of your body in just a few simple moves. If you aren't already familiar with yoga, there are plenty of tutorials online that you can watch before putting the stretches into practice; alternatively, joining a class to learn the basic moves may be a good idea. If you are particularly unfit, then it really is recommended that you attend a proper class before practicing at home, just to ensure that you know exactly how you should do the move and that you don't push yourself too far. By concentrating on your breathing as you stretch, you should be able to relax into the moves and come out of your session feeling refreshed. Ideally, you should hold each position for at least 30 seconds, but if you want to keep to just a minute, you could fit four or five positions into that time, holding each one for a few seconds each.

If you like something a little more energetic, running up and downstairs or skipping for a minute should help you to work whatever is bothering you out of your system. When you've finished, follow it up with some light stretching as your breathing slows down, then lie on the floor and relax your muscles for a few minutes.

Tips for fitting exercise into your life

Bearing in mind that you only need to exercise for short bursts in order to release the endorphins in your body, you really shouldn't have any issues fitting exercise into your life. Just getting up a few minutes early will enable you to fit in a brief exercise session. However, if it seems like too much effort, there are plenty of other ways you can fit exercise into your life and improve your state of mind at the same time.

If you usually drive to work, consider parking a bit further away than usual and walking the rest of the way. At lunchtime, instead of sitting at your desk, suggest to a colleague that you go for a walk. The combination of exercise and talking to someone about whatever is bothering you should help to clear your mind and put things into perspective. You could also try walking up stairs rather than taking the elevator. Then once you're home in the evening, put on some music and dance around the kitchen while you're preparing dinner.

Exercise should be an important part of your life, so building it into your daily routine should be something that you do anyway. Once you have a form of exercise that you enjoy, you can then use it as a form of relaxation when you are having negative thoughts. Aim to start with just a minute of exercise, but hopefully, once you've started, you'll feel encouraged to continue and will reap all the health benefits that exercise can provide.

Chapter 4:
Visualization

Sometimes classed as a form of meditation, or even hypnosis, visualization can be a powerful way of turning your negative thoughts into positive ones. It is often advocated as a way of helping people gain the success they are looking for in life, but it can also be used as a way of changing negative thoughts into positive ones. They key thing is not to aim for something that is out of reach, but rather to aim for a goal that is easily achievable and could set you on the road to greater success in the future.

What is visualization?

There are different forms of visualization. For example, in guided imagery, a practitioner helps you to create the positive images that you want to concentrate on. In neuro-linguistic programming, you work with a practitioner to retrain your mind, and it can involve verbal communication as well as images. Autogenic training aims to relax both the mind and body so that more positive thoughts come to the fore.

However, you can practice visualization without the aid of a practitioner. As with many forms of therapy, there are plenty of tutorials available online, or you may just choose to practice visualization on the basis of reading this chapter.

Does visualization actually work?

You may find it difficult to get to grips with visualization if you have never done it before. Like meditation, it can be hard to concentrate on what you want, especially if you have negative thoughts floating around your brain. However, if you persist with it, you should be able to reach the point where you can visualize something positive and focus on it for at least a minute.

Of course, you are unlikely to make yourself feel much better if you visualize something that is really out of your reach. For example, if you want to run a marathon, but can barely walk a few steps to your local shop, visualizing yourself finishing a marathon may not be practical. Instead, visualize being able to walk for 20 minutes without stopping. Once you have put that into practice, then you can start visualizing the next step, which may be to walk for an hour.

Visualization is not very different from thinking about your goals and slowly putting them into practice, but some people find it actually more helpful to put images to their goals rather than just thinking about them. If you know you are a visual learner anyway, visualization may be the right thing for you.

Steps to put visualization into practice at home

If you want a visualization to work for you at home, you'll need to get yourself in the right frame of mind first. Find somewhere quiet where you are unlikely to be disturbed and where you can be comfortable. If you think music will help you to relax, then by all means put some music on – but nothing too energetic or loud or it will distract you from concentrating on your images.

As with meditation, take some deep breaths and try to relax every part of your body. You can sit, stand, or lie down – whatever position is most comfortable for you. Once you're fully relaxed, it's time to start visualizing your goal, which is to change your state of mind from a negative one to a positive one.

Think about how you could turn your negative situation into a more positive one. Don't go too far; for example, if you have just broken up with your partner, don't visualize getting back together unless you know that there is a possibility that will happen. Instead, visualize something that will make you feel better. That could be a new haircut or an evening out with a friend.

Still breathing slowly and deeply, let the images that come to you run through your mind and try to see yourself looking and feeling happy. In times of stress and unhappiness, it can be hard to imagine feeling happy again, but try to shut out all the negative thoughts and concentrate on how you would like to be.

If you struggle with visualization, and many people do to begin with, try looking at a photograph of you when you were happy, or look at pictures of a holiday destination that you loved. Then close your eyes and think of those images. If you're more of an auditory learner than a visual one, it may help to say positive thoughts out loud in order to kick start the images.

You may find visualization unnatural to begin with, especially if you are not a visual learner. However, by following the steps in the last section, you should be able to train yourself to visualize yourself into a more positive frame of mind. In time, it will come much more naturally. The best thing of all about visualization is that you really can do it in just a minute; all you need to do is get rid of any outside distractions, close your eyes and let your mind take you to a happier place.

Chapter 5:
Benefits of Meditation

In order to understand the benefits of meditation, you must first understand how the body functions under a high amount of stress. During our day to day activities, we encounter many stressors including, but not limited to, work, children, spouses, friends, relatives, or just random events that end up affecting us in a negative way. We're under a lot more stress that we're not able to alleviate as our ancestors could. The body responds to stress in two different ways, it either makes us eat because it believes food solves everything or it produces hormones to counteract the imbalance.

Sometimes we fall into a state known as chronic stress, which has thousands of negative impacts on our body. We're unable to sleep, are more easily provoked and aroused in a negative manner, and eventually our bodies seem to think this state is normal. Meditation can alleviate these symptoms and help us regain balance in our lives.

It has the following effects on our mental and physical states:

Better Focus

Whether you're practicing just a few minutes of mindfulness every morning or evening before bed or you're engaging in a full day's worth of meditation, your focus will improve. This occurs due to the regression of stress hormones in your body that are signaling your brain to be all over the place all at once. Meditation will allow you to understand when your mind is wandering and will enable you to easily correct it.

Less Anxiety

I could tell you that you will feel less anxious because your stress hormones will reduce, but that's not the whole of it. An interesting fact is that when you meditate, you are loosening the connections of neural pathways that lead to your medial prefrontal cortex. The medial prefrontal cortex is the part of your brain that processes information that directly affects us, such as a frightening moment or something very upsetting.

When you meditate, you loosen and weaken those links so that when you experience something frightening or upsetting, you're able to step back from the situation and look at it in a more rational way.

More Creativity

It's a difficult thing to measure, but the scientists at Leiden University have done it. They ran a test to see if people who were meditating were more creative afterward, and found that those who practice open monitoring meditation were more creative when asked to perform a specific task after their meditation. Therefore, meditation will make you more creative and open to new ideas.

More Compassion

People who practice meditation on a daily basis have been shown to be more empathetic and compassionate toward others. One study took practitioners of meditation and showed them pictures of people who were joyful, those who were experiencing something awful, and those who were experiencing a neutral event. While the amygdala seems to be lessened with its effects during meditation, those who meditated on a regular basis were more responsive to the images of those who were suffering.

In 2008, a study was conducted that tested people who regularly meditated and those who did not. Those who meditated on a regular basis were more empathetic to the sounds of people who were suffering than those who did not meditate.

Improved Memory

Imagine being able to recall where you put your keys the next morning or being able to remember what you were supposed to be doing ten minutes ago. People who meditate are better able to filter out distractions as they're working, which leads to them remembering the things they want to remember, and forgetting those they don't.

Less Stress

It's the main reasons doctors and researchers have been looking into meditation for years. Mindfulness, a step in meditation, reduces the stress hormones in the body and enables us to deal with stressors in a much easier fashion. Studies have shown that those who meditate on a regular basis are more able to deal with stress in their life on a daily basis.

Increased Gray Matter

Gray matter in the brain is what is responsible for storing your memories, as well as stable emotions and a heightened sense of focus. Those who meditate on a daily basis experience an increase in gray matter in their hippocampus and frontal lobe, which translates to emotional stability and diminishing age-related cognitive decline.

Physical Benefits

Those who practice meditation regularly have reported that their blood pressure and heart rates have decreased to a normal, healthy rate. This is due to the lack of stress hormones in their systems and their ability to focus in their lives. Being able to use mediation for its physical benefits is great because it can replace several different types of medications. A study done at John Hopkins has found that mediation can actually replace antidepressants, as it is a form of brain training, not just sitting around doing nothing, despite what many people think. One thing you need to keep in mind though is mediation is not a cure for any of these physical problems, but it is something that can be used to help treat the various symptoms.

Other physical benefits include:

- Reduction of anxiety

- Better control over asthma

- Reduction of depression

- Increases ability to handle pain

- Relieves insomnia

Meditation Changes The Brain

Perhaps the biggest benefit to meditation is how it can actually change the brain. Over the past several years numerous studies have been done that detail all of the various benefits of meditation. Which those of us who enjoy meditation know that all of these benefits that are now being backed by scientific studies are actually ancient beliefs.

What is interesting about all of these studies is that they actually prove that meditation makes changes in our brains that we can measure. So, let's take a look at all of the different ways that meditation actually changes our brains.

Preserves An Aging Brain

One of these studies, which was done at UCLA, shows that mediation actually preserves an aging brain. The study gathered participants that regularly practiced meditation and those that didn't, all from a variety of different age groups. What the study found was that mediators who had been regularly mediating for about 20 years had more grey matter inside their aging brain than those who did not bother with meditation. Now the study also determined that older participants had less grey matter than the younger participants, but the loss of grey matter wasn't nearly as high when compared to mediators and non-mediators.

Decreases Mind Wandering

No matter how hard we might try to stop it we have all caught ourselves letting our mind wander from one random thought to the next. Now for some of us stopping these wandering thoughts is easier, but for those who have a hard life or those who are not currently happy with their life, stopping these wandering thoughts is a bit harder.

A study based out of Yale University has actually shown that practicing mindfulness meditation can reduce the mind wandering. How meditation does this is it helps lower the activity in the default mode network, also referred to as the DMN. This network is always active when we are not focused or thinking about something directly. Even better is for those who practice meditation it is easier for them to snap back to reality when their mind does start to wander.

Volume Changes In Certain Areas of the Brain

Now we already know that meditation can help preserve the grey matter in the brain, but what you might not realize is that it can also change the structure of the brain. Sara Lazar and a team of researchers from Harvard conducted a study in 2011 and found that after eight weeks of Mindfulness-Based Stress reduction the brain structure was altered in several different areas. The hippocampus had an increased cortical thickness, while the amygdala had a decrease in cell volume. The hippocampus focuses on learning and memory, while the amygdale deals with fear, anxiety, and stress, so these changes were obviously for the better. Lazar and her team also conducted a follow-up study that linked meditation training to an overall improvement in how people felt about themselves.

Increases Concentration

Now there are some people out there who have been diagnosed with ADD or even ADHD, kids and adults alike. These people know and understand just how difficult it can be to focus on the task at hand. However, these people are not the only ones to have problems concentrating. Everybody at some point in their life will have some kind of problem concentrating on the job they are trying to do for a variety of reasons.

Luckily, mediation can help improve your concentration, as well as your attention span. A study showed that people who practiced mediation for a period of a few weeks showed an improvement of 16 percentile points when taking the GRE. What this increase shows us is that mediation can improve concentration in a variety of areas, including school, home, and work, because it relies on focusing strongly on a certain idea, action, or even an object.

This line of though also goes along with helping kids in school. Sure it can help improve concentration, but it has also been shown to decrease the number of suspensions, improve attendance, as well as bring up a student's GPA. The reason for all of this is that meditation can be used with students who are dealing with a variety of stressors whether it's inside of school or outside forces at work. To show that mediation can help in a school setting a school district in San Francisco implemented mediation two times a day in several high risk schools and saw nothing but positive outcomes.

Improves Self-Control

One area that is not talked about too much in terms of meditation is self-control and how practicing mediation on regular basis can drastically improve your self-control. While this is great for most people, it is especially helpful for those that suffer from an addictive type personality. Learning how to meditate can help people overcome even the most serious of addictions. One study shows that people who participate in mindfulness mediation had a higher quitting rate with smoking during and 17 weeks after quitting when compared to those who used a conventional method. Theory has it that meditation helps overcome addiction because it teaches you how to handle the craving, you simply experience and then just deal with it.

Now that you're aware of the benefits of meditation let's take a look at the different types so that you can figure out which form of meditation you'd like to try first!

Chapter 6:
Types of Meditation

There are five main types of meditation with numerous sub-types underneath of them. These five types include concentration, reflective, mindfulness, heart-centered, and creative or visualization. All of the aforementioned benefits can be attained with these five different types; however, you may want to explore each type to figure out which one works best for you.

Concentration Meditation

Concentration meditation is all about eradicating distractions from the mind. It's the type of meditation commonly mentioned when someone is asked about the subject of meditation, and brings about a picture of a man sitting in the lotus position with his hands on his knees and eyes closed. This type of meditation can be difficult to master because it involves stopping your thought process and being in a state of complete silence mentally.

Popular forms of concentration meditation include Zen, Transcendental, Om, Samadhi, and Chakra Meditation.

Zen Meditation

Zen meditation is the classic picture of meditation. It's all about sitting down on a Zafu or a meditation pillow, or sitting in a straight-backed chair, closing the eyes, and focusing on the breaths and what is in the mind. It's simply sitting and being. This form of meditation does not have a focus as it's meant to clear your mind completely. It's accomplished by sitting in the lotus position on your pillow, taking in deep breaths and counting those breaths.

Transcendental Meditation

Another popular form of meditation that is meant to quiet the mind, transcendental meditation uses a mantra assigned to you by an instructor. You then repeat that mantra either out loud if you're not in a classroom setting or in your mind if you're in public. This mantra is a meaningless noise or sound that you repeat in order to become one with the universe and quiet the mind.

Om Meditation

Om meditation is actually transcendental meditation, but everyone uses the same mantra. The mantra is Om, pronounced 'aum'.

Samadhi

This form of meditation is a practice that attempts to bring the practitioner into an oneness with the universe and all that it holds. It's a way of quieting the mind; although, practitioners warn beginners not to try this type of meditation as it's extremely difficult to achieve. It's said that those who accomplish oneness with their focus do not want to return to the physical world.

Chakra Meditation

Chakra meditation is most often used as a way of healing and a way to quiet the mind. Chakras are the nerve endings that branch off from the spinal cord in order to feed the rest of the body. There are seven chakras in all, and the practice of meditating on them is meant to bring about balance in the body. Restoring this balance is thought to bring about good health.

Reflective Meditation

Reflective meditation is all about focusing on a question in order to train your mind to think in a disciplined manner. You must choose a question, theme, or topic in order to practice this type of meditation, and then you must train your brain to focus only on that topic. If your mind wanders, you must bring it back to what you were supposed to be thinking about.

This type of meditation will help you obtain more control over your thought processes so that you're not easily distracted.

Some questions you can try out include:

- What is the true meaning of my life?

- Who am I?

- What is my ultimate purpose in this life?

- How can I help others and remove their suffering?

Mindfulness Meditation

All forms of meditation include mindfulness; however, there are specific forms of meditation that focus on this technique more than others. It's an excellent form of meditation if you suffer from high amounts of stress or pain and want to relieve some of those symptoms. There are numerous forms of mindfulness meditation, but some of the most popular ones include vipassana, deep breathing, body scan, mindful eating, sitting meditation, and walking meditation.

Vipassana Meditation

This form of meditation allows the practitioner to see problems and complications in a clearer manner than when they were in a fully alert state. The point of this type of meditation is to be able to see things from a different point of view. The practitioner should be able to reach down into their inner being and make a connection between their mental and physical beings. This type of meditation is often used for healing the mind and the body.

Deep Breathing Meditation

This form of mindfulness meditation focuses solely on the breath. The practitioner should get into a comfortable position and breathe in and out freely. Avoid controlling the breath as this defeats the purpose of meditation. Sometimes people find it helpful to count or focus on energy entering them and escaping them as they breathe in and out.

Body Scan Meditation

Much like the deep breathing meditation, body scan meditation focuses on the feel of the body. At first, the practitioner simply acknowledges that they're feeling tense in some areas. Then they find that they're relaxing when they focus on the areas that trouble them.

Mindful Eating Meditation

Often used by those who are attempting to lose weight or simply enjoy the simpler things in life, mindful eating meditation is very easily done. It's all about focusing on the taste, texture, smell, and feel of the food as you're eating.

Sitting Meditation

Sitting meditation involves sitting in a chair or on a pillow on the floor and simply being. You don't control anything, chant or mentally repeat anything, or even focus on your breath. This form of mindfulness is all about focusing on nothing so that you let go of everything.

Walking Meditation

This form of meditation is best done somewhere that you're familiar with at first as you may fall into a meditative state and not know where you're going. This form of meditation focuses on the feel of your feet as you walk and your breaths. Once you're familiar with it, you can move on to practicing walking meditation in the grocery store, walking your dog, or simply walking around your yard.

Heart-Centered Meditation

This form of meditation is actually part of Chakra meditation; however, it only focuses on the heart chakra. The idea behind this meditation is that the practitioner will focus on loving kindness and compassion. It's supposed to heal the heart of the person practicing it as well as others. If you want to practice this technique, simply find a quiet place and focus on your heart area as you inhale and exhale deeply and smoothly.

Then visualize someone you feel needs compassion in their life and send it their way.

Creative or Visualization Meditation

Visualization meditation involves thinking about a specific quality or goal you would like to achieve. Some qualities you might choose to focus on include fearlessness, courage, humility, tenderness, joy, patience, compassion, appreciation, empathy, love, or gratitude. You may choose to focus on a goal instead that may involve a promotion at work or any other personal goal you may have in mind.

Now that you're aware of the different techniques let's talk about a few elements of meditation that are involved with the aforementioned techniques.

Chapter 7:
Elements of Meditation

There are four main elements to meditation. These fundamentals include focused attention, relaxed breathing, a quiet and peaceful setting, and a comfortable position. Let's explore these in a little more detail.

Focused Attention

Almost every form of meditation has a focus, and when it doesn't, beginners still choose a focus in order to get started. By focusing your attention on an object, mantra, body part, or mental image, you allow your mind to discard other distractions. Once you've mastered focusing on one element, then you can move on to discarding that element, too. However, that's a very difficult achievement that only master practitioners attain.

Relaxed Breathing

Whether you're focusing on your breathing, controlling it or simply practicing a form of meditation with another focal point, your breathing is important. Never should you be breathing rapidly during meditation as this bypasses the entire point of the practice. The idea is to rid ourselves of stress rather than create it with rapid breathing.

Quiet Setting

As a beginner, you're going to want to practice in a quiet setting. This element is not as important for those who are more apt at meditation as they can practice it anywhere.

However, as a beginner, you'll need to find a quiet area that's free from distractions such as television, cell phones, or radios. Try to schedule your meditation time when the kids are at school and your spouse is working. If that's not possible, simply ask for a few quiet moments alone.

Comfortable Position

Being in a comfortable position is of the utmost importance during meditation; however, you don't want to be stuck in a position that's going to make you more liable to fall asleep. If you're feeling tired, be sure to sit up during meditation. A comfortable position may include sitting on a zafu or meditation pillow with good posture, or sitting in a chair with excellent posture. Remember, you may be meditating for a long period of time and you don't want to put stress on your muscles and joints by sitting in a posture that's not good for you.

Those are the four elements of meditation that are universal in any practice. Now that you know them let's talk about a few others things that you need to know before you get started.

One of the first things that you must do before you begin practicing meditation is to determine what it is you want to get out of it. Are you going to adopt meditation to help reduce your stress levels or do you simply want to use it to relax. Meditation can be used for a variety of purposes, such as making peace with your past or simply getting in touch with your inner self. No matter the reason you are practicing meditation knowing why beforehand can help ensure your success.

As we have mentioned before finding a comfortable place is a vital part of meditation. If you are not in a comfortable place

37

you are more likely to be disrupted with constant distractions. When looking for a comfortable place find somewhere that you feel at peace. You also want to find somewhere that offers a comfortable temperature, hot, stuffy rooms might put you to sleep and rooms that are too cold make it hard to focus. Not only should the room be comfortable for you, but what you are sitting on should also provide some comfort. Many people find a soft, cushion works great for meditation, while others prefer a stool or chair. The key to picking something out aside from comfort is something that will not cause you to slouch.

Now that you have a great place to go you need to start thinking about beginning your first session. One mistake that beginners often make is eating too much right before a session, although some also make the mistake of not eating enough. You don't want to be super full before your meditation session as that can lead to you getting sleepy. On the other hand being hungry can distract you from being focused. Work on finding the perfect balance; grab a quick snack beforehand that is meant to be filling. Being hydrated is also important, but you want to make sure you don't drink so much that you have to get up in the middle of your session to go to the bathroom.

Now this next part is really going to depend on what type of meditation you are practicing. If you are practicing meditation that involves precise positions for your body, please pay no attention to what I am about to tell you. In meditation it is important that you keep your spine straight while relaxing your body so that you can avoid any kind of physical stress to your body. Keeping your posture correct allows you to sit still for extended periods of time, so remember keep your chin up and your shoulders back.

Changing position is highly recommended for meditation, as it allows you to focus on different mental energies. So instead of staying in the same position for the entire twenty minutes, switch it up. Go from cross-legged meditation to walking meditation. No matter what position you start with, do not start practicing meditation until you are calm. If your mind is going a hundred miles a minute, you will find it nearly impossible to focus. Going for a walk or even taking a bath is a great way to calm the mind before a session.

Chapter 8:
Let's Focus on Breathing

If you haven't picked up on it yet, breathing is one of the most important aspects of meditation. No matter what kind of meditation you are participating in, you will need be doing something with your breathing. In this chapter we are going to discuss just about every aspect of breathing and what kind of role it plays in meditation.

One of the main reasons why every type of meditation focuses on breathing exercises is because of how great they are at being able to relieve stress. In fact breathing exercises are used in a variety of stress relieving techniques, not just in meditation. Breathing exercises are great to use in the middle of a stressful situation, as they can help you start calming down immediately. Not only that but since they help you reverse your body's response to stress, you won't have to worry about any side effects related to chronic stress.

One of the reasons why they come so highly recommended in a variety of different sources is because of how effective they are, but how easy and simple they are too do for everyone who tries them. Not only that but breathing exercises are amazing because of how quickly they work and the fact that you can literally do them anywhere, unlike yoga positions. If that isn't enough to convince you about the importance of breathing exercises how about how easy they are to master and to learn all about how to do them you simply have to continue reading this book.

Breathing Exercises Benefits

Not only are breathing exercises easy, they are also quite beneficial. Breathing exercises do far more than just relieve your stress. As I mentioned earlier breathing exercises can actually reverse your body's response to stress. This is beneficial because if the responses are not reversed quickly you will end up suffering from something called chronic stress. And, let me tell you the problems that chronic stress causes on your body is not something you want to ever experience.

While helping with stress is probably the biggest benefit you will receive, breathing exercises provide many other benefits for your body. Slowing down your breathing promotes a state of deep relaxation, which can also help relieve any feelings of tension. Breathing exercises can also help treat headaches, problems concentrating, hyperventilation, depression, anxiety, panic attacks, and even heart disease.

Now what you always need to keep in mind is that breathing exercises should never replace a doctor's care, especially for serious conditions. Instead breathing exercises should simply play a role in your treatment plan.

Best Time To Use Breathing Exercises

As I have already mentioned, breathing exercises play a big role in meditation, but they can also be used on their own. However, what you need to keep in mind is that using breathing exercises in conjunction with meditation is your best choice, as the two of these methods together are going to work the best to combat any kind of stress you are feeling. You can use both meditation and breathing exercises when you are feeling overwhelmed, when you want to think more clearly, or even when you simply want to slow things down a bit because you are feeling frustrated. Combining meditation and deep breathing exercises is a great way to help center yourself even during the heat of the moment.

Types of Breathing Exercises

There are several different breathing exercises that you can use in combination with meditation or even by themselves. No breathing exercise is really better than the other, but people do have their own personal preferences. What you need to do is look them over, try them out, and then find the ones that works best for you. You might even find one type to work better for immediate stress relief, while another might work to help you center yourself.

Basic Breathing

Basic breathing exercises are a great way to help relax and chase away stress. The best part is they can be done everywhere, by just about everybody. To get started all you need to do is stop what you are doing and find a comfortable position, whether it is sitting or standing it doesn't matter.

Once you are comfortable start in by breathing in through your nose. As you are breathing in slowly count to five inside your head. Once you get to five you are going to slowly exhale through your mouth. But, now you are going to count to eight as you let the air out. Continue these basic steps until you feel like yourself again.

Deep Breathing

One of the great things about deep breathing exercises is that you can do them on your own or with a partner, including your children. In fact, teaching your children about deep breathing at a young age can help them better manage stress, which can affect children without you even realizing it.

If you plan to teach your children about deep breathing exercises you will need to sit them down and talk to them about what you are doing. How detailed you go in the conversation will actually depend on how old the child is. One of the first things both you and your child need to learn is how to breathe properly for deep breathing exercises. You do NOT want your shoulders or chest to move while you are breathing, you simply want your stomach going in and out, also known as diaphragm breathing.

Once you have the breathing figured out and slowed down is the time to focus on longer breathing. Ideally you will want to breathe in and hold it inside for six seconds and then slowly let it out. What you want to avoid is letting all of your air out in one huge gush. As you exhale it helps to count as you exhale, ideally you want the exhale to take six to eight seconds.

The best part about deep breathing exercises is the more you practice the better you get. If you practice often enough, deep breathing will become second nature and whenever you are faced with a stressful situation you will find yourself naturally reverting to this stress reliving method.

Visualization Breathing

This method combines breathing exercises along with visualization, which is a great combination for stress relief. The best part is you really only need about 5 minutes to see some pretty great results.

With visualization breathing you need to sit and relax with your eyes closed. As you sit there allow your breathing to slow down and become deeper. Always breath from your diaphragm not your shoulders or chest, only your stomach should be moving when you breath. Sit quietly until your breathing has become natural.

Once you are breathing naturally, you can start the visualization process. Each time you breathe in picture the relaxing breath coming in and flowing through your entire body. When you let your breathe out picture all of your stress going out with it. You can also change what you are visualizing to something that works better for you. The key to visualizing is to completely relax your body. Continue with this breathing exercise for at least five minutes, but you can go longer.

Bath Meditation Breathing

As you might have guessed based on its name bath meditation breathing is done in the bathtub. Many people find this to be a great form of meditation, as you get all of the benefits of meditation, but you can also quickly relax sore or tired muscles, as well as enjoy a very relaxing atmosphere. So with how amazing bath meditation sounds, let's talk about how to take advantage of it.

With bath meditation you need to set aside at least 15 minutes where you will not be disturbed, some people prefer longer, but that is entirely up to you. As you are getting the bath water ready, add some aromatherapy bath products so you can really reap the rewards. Lavender can help you relax, while peppermint can help you feel more alert and focused. Adding aromatherapy bath products gives you extra stress relief without even trying.

Once the bath water is ready to go, all you have to do is hope in and start relaxing. In terms of breathing you need to focus on slowing down your breathing. Your stomach should rise and fall with each breath you take in and let out, not your chest and shoulders. As you focus on your breathing pay attention to how your body is feeling. How does the water feel on your skin, just focus on the present moment and no random thoughts.

Karate Meditation Breathing

This is probably one of the most commonly used breathing exercises in meditation because of how easy it is to pick up. If you want to give it a try you are going to first need to get yourself into a comfortable position, some prefer sitting with their feet under their buttocks with their knees placed on the floor, while others prefer sitting crossed legged. No matter how you sit just make sure you are comfortable and that your back is straight and your head is up with relaxed shoulders. Your eyes should be closed, but looking forward from behind your lids.

Now it's time to work on the breathing aspect. Take in a deep cleansing breath. Your shoulders should still be relaxed while your stomach expands. Hold the breath in for six seconds and then slowly exhale. This should be repeated two more time and then you return to normal breathing. While breathing normally you should breathe in through your nose and out through your mouth. At no time should your shoulders be moving up and down, your stomach should be expanding with each inhale and deflating with each exhale.

When breathing you want your stomach to do the work rather than your shoulders, as that is the natural way to breathe.

Breathing naturally allows for a bigger lung capacity, which helps provide more oxygen to the blood. One thing to watch out for is breathing too fast or even too slowly, you want to breathe normally but take deeper breaths.

Chapter 9:
Practicing Basic Meditation

Do you remember the meditation techniques I mentioned in Chapter Two? Well, you're going to get some first-hand experience with some of the easier techniques in this chapter. First, you'll need to get into an open state of mind, and then perform the following.

Pre-Meditation Techniques

Find Your Environment

You'll need a peaceful environment to begin with so as to get the practice underway and not become frustrated by too many loud distractions. Try to find an area that's private so that you're not disturbed while you're meditating, and be sure that it's free from tons of outside stimuli. You can even use a walk-in closet if you'd like! Here are some tips to make your space free from as many distractions as you can.

- Turn off all electronics such as your television, cell phone, noisy appliances, radios, and laptops. You don't want to be interrupted by a beep letting you know you have a new text message or e-mail as it is counterproductive. In addition, you can try to turn on some soft, calming music or a small water fountain in order to block out other noises.

- Your meditation area does not need to be utterly silent, so don't use ear plugs. The idea is to be able to dampen your outside stimuli in the beginning so that you can learn the technique, and then you can slowly introduce outside stimuli to your routine.

- Meditating outside is actually an excellent idea because it allows you to get into nature and experience exterior stimuli, yet nature sounds are usually very calming and peaceful.

- If you are using a room inside of your home make sure it is a room that you do not use for things like sleeping, working, or exercising. Sometimes finding a room can be hard, as you might be limited on space, so opt for a corner of the room that you can block off and set up for mediation.

- Adding candles and other spiritual knick knacks can help create the perfect meditation environment.

Wear Appropriate Clothing

You're just working against yourself if you're wearing uncomfortable clothing as you're attempting to meditate. Therefore, pick clothing that is not physically tight or restrictive. Loose clothing will help you feel relaxed. And don't wear shoes!

- If you're someplace cool, then wear a loose sweater or sweatshirt.

- If you're somewhere that you can't change your clothes, try just taking off your jacket, removing your belt, and taking off your shoes.

Find a Time Period

Before you even begin meditating, you need to decide how long you're going to be meditating. Most practitioners may recommend a good twenty minutes twice a day, but beginners should start with just five minutes once a day in order to create the habit of meditation.

- Try to meditate at the same time every day and make it part of your routine. If you wish to bring yourself to the next level with meditation you need to make it a formal practice. Most experts recommend to take things to the next level you need to meditate at least two times a day.

- Stick with your timeframe and don't let frustration get the better of you. If a timeframe isn't working, switch it to another time but don't stop meditating altogether!

- Don't check your watch while you're meditating because this is counterproductive. Instead, set a gentle alarm on your otherwise silent cell phone.

- When picking a time to meditate the morning is honestly the best time period, the earlier the better. The reason why early mornings are best is because it is quieter and your mind isn't filled with nearly as many thoughts. Not to mention the chance of you being disrupted is less because most of your household will still be sleeping. Best way to make time to meditate in the morning is to wake up half an hour earlier each morning.

Stretch

You're going to be sitting in one area for a specific amount of time, so it's best to rid yourself of any tension you're feeling beforehand. Stretch out your entire body and be sure to work out any kinks before you sit down to meditate, else you might focus on your sore spots rather than on your meditation.

- Stretch your neck and shoulders, especially if you're an office worker who sits in front of a chair all day.

- Stretch your legs and your back because you need optimal blood flow to these areas in order to be comfortable.

- Stretching is an important part of meditation as it allows you to bring more attention to your body as it allows you to really look in at your body as you focus on each muscle as you stretch.

Find a Comfortable Position

As aforementioned, you need a comfortable position in order to focus on your meditation. If you're flexible, you can try the lotus position as described below.

- Lotus Position

  o Fold or cross your legs like you may have done as a child and put the tops of your feet on the opposite, inner thighs.

  o Sit up straight and bring your shoulder blades back a little in order to square them.

o   Rest your hands on your knees or form a circle with your index finger and thumb and rest the outside of your palm on your knees.

- Half Lotus Position

    o   Cross your legs as if you were a child and rest the outside of your feet on the ground.

    o   Sit up straight with good posture.

    o   Rest your hands on your knees.

If you're not as flexible, you may choose to sit in a chair or lie down on your back. The most important aspect about this is that you're comfortable; otherwise, you'll be focusing on your discomforts rather than your meditation.

Keep Your Eyes Closed

While you can perform meditation with your eyes open or closed, it's best to start with them closed if you're a beginner. By doing this, you are blocking any visual stimuli that's external and allowing yourself to focus easier.

Now some beginners report that they have a hard time meditating with their eyes closed. However, keeping your eyes opening can be a challenge as well. If you are having difficulty with your eyes closed you can try using a candle to help you keep your focus. With the candle lit you can focus your attention on the flame and use it as your point of focus. This can prove to be quite powerful as you use the flame as a visual cue to strengthen your attention and focus.

Once you've practiced meditation long enough, you can attempt it with your eyes open. Sometimes it's best to use the open-eyed method in order to keep from falling asleep during meditation or concentrating too hard. In a few rare cases, people have reported disturbing mental images while they're meditating and they're more comfortable with their eyes open.

Meditation Techniques

Deep Breathing

This is by far the easiest and the most universally used beginner's technique for meditation. It is also the starting point for just about every style of meditation. Deep breathing is going to slow down your heart rate, focus your mind, and will help you relax all of your muscles. Breathing meditation obviously focuses on your breathing, but it doesn't control your breathing patterns. To get started, simply find a comfortable position and focus on the rising and falling of your abdomen during breathing.

- Do not focus on your breathing so much that you're passing judgment on it, such as how long it was or if it was too short. Simply acknowledge that you're breathing.

- A good image to use is a lotus flower on your abdomen that opens when you inhale and closes as you exhale.

- Do not become discouraged if your mind brings up other topics. Simply steer it back gently and without judgment to your breathing.

Mantra

You may choose your own mantra or you may obtain one from an instructor, either or is fine. Mantra meditation is very common and focuses on a sound, word or phrase that you repeat until you silence the mind.

- You should start with a simple word such as peace or one. You may choose to use the traditional 'Om' mantra.

- A mantra is an instrument that creates vibrations within your mind.

- You should repeat the mantra to yourself repeatedly, silently and not worry if your mind wanders. Simply bring it back gently and without judgment.

- If you enter a deeper level of meditation, you may not need to repeat the mantra.

Trataka

This form of meditation is rather common and usually practiced alone. It involves using a visual in front of the practitioner, something that they can focus on such as a candle. The object can be anything, but I'm going to use a candle in my example.

- Place the object within your line of sight at your eye level so that you do not have to look up or down.

- Gaze at the object until it takes up your entire vision. If you're using a candle, be careful not to gaze too long.

- Gaze for twenty to thirty seconds and then close the eyes gently and see the candle flame or the outline of the object behind your eyelids.

- Focus on that outline.

- When the outline has faded, open the eyes and repeat.

- Do not practice Trataka for more than three months daily with a candle flame. Change it to another object to avoid damaging your retinas.

Visualization

Some choose to visualize a place of tranquility and peace while others try to visualize themselves completing a goal. In order to attain inner peace and happiness, we're going to focus on the place of tranquility for example purposes.

- Visualize a place that is comfortable for you. This can a beach, a meadow, a sitting room with a fire roaring, or anywhere else that makes you feel at peace.

- When you're in your sanctuary, simply explore it and look at your surroundings. You do not need to actively create anything as it's already there in your mind.

- Allow your surroundings to expand and become more real by *feeling* them with your five senses: touch, taste, smell, hearing, and sight.

- When you're feeling calmer and ready to leave, just take a few deep breaths and open your eyes slowly.

- You can use the same space or you can change it every time you meditate.

Body Scan

If you're looking for a way to become comfortable and relax your body as well as your mind, try the body scan technique.

- Close your eyes and focus on the toes. Feel how they are relaxing and are relaxed. Then focus on your calves and up to your hips and feel how those muscles are relaxing. Keep continuing up your body until you're at the crown of your head.

- Once you've achieved relaxation of your entire body, take a few moments to feel how relaxed you are, and then come out of it with a few deep breaths.

Heart Chakra

Heart chakra meditation is focused on love, peace, compassion and acceptance of yourself and others. You can find your heart chakra in the center of your chest.

- To start, make sure your eyes are closed and then rub your palms together in order to create friction and heat. Once they're warm, place the right palm on your heart chakra and the left palm over your right hand.

- Now, breathe in deeply and then when you exhale, say the word 'yum.' This is the vibration that's associated with your heart chakra. When you say the word 'yum,' imagine that an energy that is glowing and green is coming from your chest and entering your hands.

- The green energy symbolizes love and life. When you feel that you're ready, pull your palms away from your chest and face them outward so that you send love to your friends and family.

- Once you're finished, take a few deep breaths and come out of the meditative state.

Walking

Walking meditation is used as a way to break up long sessions of sitting meditation, or as a good way to practice meditation when out in the public. It's all about getting in touch with the movement of your feet and how they're connecting with the earth. If you can't seem to sit still during meditation, walking meditation might be an excellent alternative for you.

- If you can, remove your shoes. You should be in a place that is large enough that you can take seven paces forward without needing to turn.

- Keep your posture good and hold your head up so that you are looking forward. Clasp your hands together in front of you and hold them in front of your chest as if you were in prayer. Then take a deliberate step forward and pause. Concentrate on the feeling of that step.

- Only one foot should be moving at a time.

- Once you've reached the end of seven paces, stop and put your feet together. Pivot on your right foot and turn around. Now, continue walking in the opposite direction and use the same deliberate movements as you did before.

- Only focus on the movement of your feet and nothing else as you're walking. Try to clear your mind and be aware of your feet touching the earth or floor beneath you.

Useful Mediation Techniques and Tips

Practicing meditation is very useful for almost every aspect of your life. Like we mentioned in the beginning of this book meditation can help you physically, mentally, and emotionally. However, in order for you to fully experience the benefits of meditation you are going to need to make sure you are practicing it correctly.

One thing that you might have noticed when you first started meditating is how your mind first reacted. If you are like most people first starting out with meditation you probably noticed that your mind was going all over the place, you probably had a mixture of a bunch of jumbled thoughts. What you need to realize is these jumbled thoughts that run rampant across your mind is a normal for beginners, so don't get too upset with yourself. Instead of stressing over this what you need to do is follow some simple tips that are designed to help you meditate so you can find the peace that you are looking for.

#1 Focus

One of the hardest things to achieve when it comes to meditation is focus, after all many of us practice mediation as a way to improve our focus. All too often we find ourselves on autopilot, we let our minds wander while we are doing something routine and once we are done we have no memory of what happened in between. So to improve this, what you need to focus on where you are at during meditation. Zero in on something, such as your breathing, so that you are aware of what is going on around you. You need to understand that you are meditating for a reason. Meditation is not a passive activity, it is an active process. You have to be fully engaged in the process in order for it to work.

One thing to really watch out for is your interest fading as this can affect your ability to focus. If you really feel like giving meditation up because you feel it no longer fits into your life, you need to rethink your feelings. When you start feeling this way you really need meditation, as chances are you are losing the ability to focus in a variety of areas in your life.

#2 Breathing

One of the best ways to keep yourself focused and in the present is to zero in on your breathing. When focusing on your breathing you are anchoring yourself to the present moment, as you are focused on what is going on right now. With your breathing there is nothing special that you need to do, all you have to do is breath naturally and pay attention to the breaths as they go in and out.

#4 Settling In

Sometimes if you are having a hard time calming yourself down or getting into the groove of meditation you can count your breaths. Now if you do decide to try this out, which we highly recommend as it is an ancient meditation technique, you need to realize that you don't just start counting from one and go up from there. To count your breaths you start with one on your first out breath, but you stop at four. After you get to four, you simply return back to the number one and go back up to four again. Anytime you find your thoughts wandering or you feel like you are not in control of your mind, simply start counting and one.

#5 Chase Away Random Thoughts

Meditation is not about your thoughts, you shouldn't be focused or thinking about any kind of thought. If you happen to find thoughts pushing their way up to the surface of your mind you need to turn your attention away from them in a calm manner. Don't try to shove them aside, as that can cause you to lose focus, simply acknowledge that they are there, but return your focus back to your breathing.

#6 Dealing With Emotions

If you are dealing with your emotions consciously getting into the proper place to practice meditation can be next to impossible. Dealing with any kind of emotions, especially those that illicit a strong response, can make it hard to settle yourself down, as these emotions constantly play through your mind. To help settle yourself the best bet is to deal with the emotions by focusing on the way they are making your body feel. For example, the feeling of rage inside your belly or the tightness in your shoulders. Focusing on how your body is feeling helps let go of the feelings without dealing with the stress caused by the stories themselves.

One thing that you are going to be dealing with, especially if you are just getting started with meditation, is frustration. Most beginners are easily frustrated when they find quieting he mind isn't as easy as they had hoped, even people who have been meditating for years feel frustrated at times, the difference is they have learned to deal with it effectively. If you start feeling frustrated acknowledge the feelings, but then let them go. Turn your focus to your breathing once again and as you exhale let the frustrated feelings go out with each breath.

#7 Session length

There is no right or wrong time frame when it comes to meditation, how long your session lasts is purely up to you. However, some people find it hard to figure out a time frame that works for them. Most experts recommend you start with a ten minute session and only move up from there if you feel like you didn't sit long enough or you felt it was too short. Starting off slow is the best way to go, as you get further into meditation you will find it is easier to extend your sessions.

#8 Noise levels

Some people prefer total silence when they are meditating, while others prefer some background noise. Many professionals recommend silence, as that is seriously the best option out there. Silence is considered the best choice because you can totally focus on what your mind is doing, plus it is easier and faster to calm yourself in silence. If you prefer background noise make sure it is super low and is considered meditation music.

#9 Experiment

Most of us have some kind of general idea implanted in our heads about what meditation should look like. Now whether that image is sitting cross legged on the floor with our hands on our knees and our eyes closed or something else, all it is, is an image we have engraved in our brains. Meditation is not about the image, it is about focusing on the present moment. Don't be afraid to try different positions and techniques, the more options you try the more likely you are to find the style you are most comfortable with. You can even mix things up a bite, try a meditation technique and lay on the ground instead of sitting. Open your eyes rather than keep them closed. Don't be afraid to try new things, as you never know what is going to work for you.

#10 Really Feel Your Body Parts

There are numerous meditation exercises that you can adopt for your everyday life that will help you become a master of meditation. However, one of the easiest ones that requires no additional thought is to feel your body parts as soon as you notice the meditative state starting to take hold. You will know you are in the right state of mind as your thoughts will have quieted down. As soon as that happens focus your attention on your feet and really try to feel your feet in the moment. Work your way up from your feet, making sure to take notice of each and every body part.

#11 Pay Attention To The Small Things

Paying attention to the small things is a great tip for beginners because it can help ensure your success. All too often beginners feel frustrated at the slow progress or how easily distracted they are. What you need to do is pay attention to the smallest details, including physical movement no matter how slight. Acknowledging these small details can help you feel a sense of accomplishment and move you away from the feelings of frustration.

One thing that you need to keep in mind is that meditation is not just something that you can take up temporarily; you need to be in it for the long haul. If you truly want to benefit from meditation you have to practice every day for the duration. Even when it gets frustrating all you can do is do your best, it is what it is, don't stress over what happens during your session afterwards.

Now that you're familiar with some beginner's meditation techniques let's take a look at how you can incorporate different meditation styles into your daily life in order to be less stressed and happier.

Chapter 10:
Is Music Meditation Worth It

In Chapter Two we discussed the different types of meditation. However, one style of mediation that you will not find listed in Chapter Two is music meditation. One of the reasons why it isn't included in the chapter is because there is no official style of meditation called music mediation.

Before we talk about how to practice music meditation, let's quickly go over what it is and how it can be beneficial for you. Music meditation is pretty much what it sounds like; you practice meditation while you are listening to music. How this kind of meditation came about was somebody had the idea of putting music and mediation together because of their stress relieving abilities.

It has long been understood that listening to music can soothe you. Hence the saying about music soothing the savage beast. And as we have learned throughout the course of this book meditation is a very good stress management tool. So, if you put the two of these together you are getting even better stress relief as you are getting two the best of both worlds.

So, if you are interested in music meditation, which not everybody is, as they prefer silence to noise, here is a quick overview of how you can effectively practice music meditation.

Step One: Pick Your Music

The most important thing to do when practicing this style of meditation is to pick your music. Now obviously you are going to want to pick music that you enjoy listening too. After all the idea behind picking out your music is opting for something that is going to help you relax. Something to keep in mind when choosing your meditation music is to stay away from music that has words, as you can find yourself focusing on the words of the song rather than on the present moment. You also want to opt for something with a slower tempo, as too fast of a tempo can prove to be distracting. The goal in meditation is to turn off your conscious mind.

Step Two: Get Started

Once you have your music playing you are ready to get started. To start meditating to your music you will want to sit in a comfortable position, just like all other meditation techniques. Once you are seated comfortably you need to let yourself relax, let all of the tension from your body go. To do this close your eyes and focus on your breathing, you should be breathing from your diaphragm.

Step Three: Focus

Once you have relaxed all you need to do is focus in on the music. Now what you will find happening is your mind will focus on other random thoughts or even on the actual music itself. When this happens you need to redirect your thoughts. What you need to be focusing on is the sound of the music and how it makes you feel in the present moment.

Step Four: Continue For 20 Minutes

You are going to want to practice this for at least 20 minutes, which is how long an average meditation session lasts. Each and every time you find yourself getting distracted you need to refocus yourself. The whole point to meditating is to learn how to quiet down your inner voice. Using music you can let yourself become one with the music; the more involved you get in it the faster you will find yourself relaxing.

Useful Tips You Can Use With Music Meditation

One thing that people find hard about meditation in general is achieving a full length session, for many beginners 20 minutes is just too long to start with. Instead of trying to start off with 20 minutes, limit yourself to a certain number of songs, say 3 or 4. Once you feel you have those pretty well mastered you can increase the number of songs until you are able to sit and meditate for at least 20 minutes, longer if you prefer.

Finding the perfect music for meditation can be quite a challenge. There are plenty of websites that you can visit for a play list of songs that are ideal for meditation; there are also some apps that you can download that come complete with meditation music. If you are having a hard time relaxing or find yourself easily distracted by the music, you need to consider switching to a different type of music.

Always remember that if you find yourself getting distracted, especially in the beginning, don't put yourself down over it. This is completely normal, especially for beginners. What you need to do instead is congratulate yourself for even noticing that you were distracted and then refocus your attention once again to being in the present moment.

Chapter 11:
Aromatherapy and Meditation

Over the past several years aromatherapy has gained national attention. In fact, everyday more and more people are purchasing aromatherapy products to help with a variety of issues. Aromatherapy has gained so much popularity that you can even find the most basic of products inside your local grocery store.

Research has been done to help show how beneficial aromatherapy is, but even with all of these studies done it is still not a proven method of stress relief. However, most people have discovered that using various aromatherapy products in conjunction with their meditation provides better results than just using aromatherapy or even meditation alone. One of the best things about using aromatherapy along with meditation is it has no known side effects and can be used passively. What this means for you is you can use it while participating in other activities and still benefit from the results.

So, if you have decided to give aromatherapy a try along with meditation, you might be wondering where to start. There are several products on the market you can try, what scents you choose is going to be based on what you like, as well as a little research into what you are trying to achieve. So, before you get started let's quickly go over some of the more popular products that you can buy.

Candles

These are probably one of the most popular options because of how easy they are to use. Simply purchase the candle or candles, light them, and let them burn. When purchasing the candle you want to make sure you smell them before buying them. You want a potent one. The more scent it gives off the better chance you have of filling the entire room with that scent.

Diffusers

Now if you are going to consider this option you need to know that a diffuser requires you to use essential oils as well. With a diffuser you place a few drops of an essential oil into the diffuser, which the diffuser then circulates the scent through the air. There are several different options for diffusers, some require the use of candles, and others rely on batteries or another form of power.

Body Products

Body products include things like lotions and topical essential oils. One of the benefits to these kinds of products is the scents literally follow you around all day. Lotions can be rubbed on the hands or over your entire body. Essential oils can be dabbed onto pulse points for hours of relief.

Incense

This is similar to candles, as in you have to burn the product to reap the benefits. However, one downfall to incense compared to candles is how much smoke incense produces. On the upside though, a stick of incense is potent enough to scent a large room.

As we mentioned earlier combining aromatherapy and meditation is a great way to relieve stress. Both aromatherapy and meditation are used to help quiet the mind, as well as relax the body, so using them together gives you twice the benefits. One of the great things about the numerous aromatherapy products is that they can be incorporated into your regular meditation sessions without very much effort.

Using incense or candles is a great way to incorporate aromatherapy into your session. Once you are ready to begin your session light the stick of incense or even the candle and get into a comfortable position. As you are sitting there focus on the smoke that is slowly drifting up towards the ceiling. Don't think about anything else, just concentrate on the smoke, notice the different patterns the smoke is making or even the various paths it is following as it climbs higher and higher.

One of the benefits to using candles or incense along with meditation is it gives you something physical to focus on. And if you feel your thoughts start to wander, which is going to happen especially in the beginning, you can redirect yourself by focusing in on the trails of smoke. Bear in mind that if using incense sticks the smoke can become quite intense. The last thing you want to do is let the smoke get too close to your face. When using incense for aromatherapy meditation make sure to do so in a well-ventilated room. And never directly inhale the smoke!

What is important to remember with aromatherapy and meditation is in order for them to be effective you will need to pick the right scents. You will want a scent that is pleasant to you, but you will also need to research the different properties of each scent before you decide to use it. Experts recommend using lavender, peppermint, and sage for aromatherapy meditation. Lavender is known for its calming properties, while sage is more about cleansing, and peppermint is great for mental focus.

Chapter 12:
Chocolate Meditation

Now let's be honest here who doesn't like chocolate, sop just the thought of something called chocolate meditation is enough to get most of us excited. When people think of chocolate as a way to reduce stress they surely don't put it together with meditation. Majority of people view meditation as a breathing exercise that can be used to center and focus the mind to help relieve stress. While this is true in most cases, meditation comes in all different styles and chocolate meditation happens to be one of them.

Chocolate meditation is probably the most delicious form of meditation that you will ever find. In fact, it is so good that many people have quickly adopted it as heir favorite form of meditation. The best part of chocolate meditation is it is convenient and easy enough for beginners to adopt. However, it is also effective enough hat people who have been meditating for years have no guilt about giving it a try. And most of them are surprised to learn that it is as effective as other styles of meditation, and it provides you with the same benefits of "proven" meditation methods.

Getting Started With Chocolate Meditation

One of the benefits to chocolate meditation is how simple it is, all you need to do is set aside 5 to 15 minutes in your day. This time can replace your old meditation time or you can set aside a new block of time.

To start you are going to need a piece of chocolate. What kind of chocolate you choose will depend on your personal preference, but remember dark chocolate has plenty of benefits on its own. You don't need a big piece of chocolate; in fact a small handful of chocolate chips is plenty for this technique. If you are going with a square of chunk of chocolate you will want something that is considered bite sized or just a tad bit larger.

Now as you sit there take a few deep, cleansing breaths and allow your body to relax. You don't want to start the meditation process until you are as physically relaxed as possible. So breathe in the good and exhale the bad.

Once you are relaxed you are ready to begin chocolate meditation, which you can do with your eyes open or shut, whatever you feel most comfortable with. To begin take a small bite of your chocolate, such as a single chocolate chip. Let the chocolate sit on your tongue and slowly melt inside your mouth. As the chocolate begins to melt take notice of the flavors that are hitting your tongue. Absorb yourself in the chocolate melting, in what you are experiencing right now. Continue the deep breathing as you focus on everything that is happening inside your mouth.

Once the chocolate has melted or as you need to swallow focus on how everything feels going down your throat. Once you have swallowed take notice of the emptiness inside your mouth. Then slowly lift your arm, paying attention to every aspect of the movement, to take a second bite of chocolate. Let yourself feel how the chocolate feels in between your fingers. Upon taking the second bite of chocolate again pay attention to how everything feels as it melts on your tongue.

Continue with this process until the chocolate is gone. Make sure that while you are eating the chocolate that you are savoring every single moment. Then play the moments in your head randomly throughout the day. Replaying the savoring feelings can help you relax.

With chocolate meditation you don't have to eat a ton of chocolate to feel the effects. In fact, if you are doing it like you are supposed to you won't be eating much of it at all. With chocolate meditation the key is to take small bites and savor each piece as it melts inside your mouth. You can even use other foods that are considered savory foods, which is great for those who have issues with chocolate or sugar.

Mindful Eating Tips

Chocolate meditation is a form of mindful eating. Along with the meditation benefits, mindful eating can also help with weight loss. Here are some tips that you can follow to ensure mindful eating is successful for you.

Hands

Something as simple as using your less dominant hand to eat your meal can alter the entire feeling of the meal. By using your less dominant hand you will end up having to work harder to eat a simple meal, which will allow you to appreciate it that much more. The harder you have to work the more attention you are going to pay to the meal; you are going to appreciate every single bite that you take. Using your opposite hand also lowers the chance of you mindless shoving food in your mouth, you will be more likely to notice that are full and stop eating before you are over full.

Mindful Meal

If you really want to work yourself hard try eating an entire meal in a mindful mindset. To do this you are going to have to focus on all of the sensations each bite of food brings you. Pay attention to the feelings in your mouth, throat, and stomach, but also pay attention to the other parts of your body. Focus on the movements your arms and hands make as you bring each bite to your mouth. The feeling of your jaw closing and your teeth coming together as you chew the food. In mindful eating you can even pay attention to the thoughts that pop into your head, as you savor each bite. The key to mindful meals is to eat slowly and pay attention to everything.

Chapter 13:
Meditation For Perfectionists

Meditation is a great way to get in touch with your inner self, it is also a great way to calm yourself and relive stress. One of the reasons why meditation is so popular is because of how easy it is to master, plus you can pretty much do it anywhere without anybody knowing what you are doing. However, not everybody finds meditation easy to master, namely those people known as perfectionists.

Now the funny thing about meditation being difficult for perfectionists to grasp is that it is these kinds of people who would actually benefit the most from meditation. In fact, perfectionists often become some of the most dedicated, well once they master it that is. Luckily, there are plenty of different options for perfectionists to try, so that they too can become masters of meditation.

As with all types of meditation the first step is to sit back, close your eyes, and let your body relax. This part is something even the worst perfectionist can master. It's the second part of meditation that perfectionists struggle with the most.

Once you are relaxed you are going to need to work on clearing your mind, which for you is probably easier said than done. What you are going to need to do is work on thinking about absolutely nothing, which often means anything and everything will pop into your mind simply because you don't want it too. One easy way to clear your mind is to focus on something, such as your breathing or the way the chair feels against your body.

One of the biggest problems perfectionists have is when thoughts enter their mind after they think they have cleared their mind. What you need to realize is that it is normal for thoughts to randomly enter your mind, even after you have started focusing on your breathing. Just because thoughts enter your mind you are not doing meditation wrong, which is what many perfectionists often think. If you start thinking that you are doing it wrong you tend to cause more thoughts to swirl through your mind. What you need to do is let your thoughts go. Praise yourself for noticing the thoughts coming in and then release those thoughts. Viewing it this way helps you feel like you are on the right track.

One of the most important things to remember as a perfectionist is that in order to master meditation you are going to have to practice it on a regular basis. This is actually where perfectionists are better than your average person because they are going to give t their all until they have it fully mastered. When practicing meditation do so several times a week and slowly work your way up to every day.

One problem many perfectionists have is they set the goal too high and then either put it off or simply give up because it's too hard. Setting a smaller goal, such as three times a week, allows perfectionists to start off small and achieve the goal allowing them to work up towards the next goal rather than giving up.

Another problem perfectionist's face is putting too much pressure on themselves; they tend to expect perfect results every time. That kind of pressure often leads to giving up. Don't expect too much out of your first meditation sessions. Don't expect your sessions to last a half hour at a time. Instead set goals of five or ten minutes and as you master the process increase the time. And, remember if one type of meditation doesn't work for you, you don't have to give up. Simply move on and try a different type until you find one that works best for you.

Troubleshooting the Stressfulness of Meditation

Now meditation is supposed to help you relieve stress, not create stress. However, for some people out there the simple act of practicing meditation is so stressful that they simply give up. By giving up on meditation you are never going to realize how beneficial meditation is to your entire being, so instead of giving up let's look at some of the most troublesome areas of meditation and figure out what you can do to help relieve the stress associated with them.

Silence Causes You To Think Of Stuff That Needs To Get Done

This probably shouldn't be too surprising, but this is one of the most common problems with meditation. People find that when they sit there in the silence their minds wander towards all of the things that they need to do. These people feel that they can't clear their mind because they have so much going on. The good news is that even people well practiced in meditation have trouble with this one at times, so you are not alone in facing this problem.

Now it is true that some people find it easier to clear their thoughts than others, which could be related to some people simply have more on their minds than others. Some people can let all of these thoughts go, but many of us struggle with it and it affects our meditation because we feel like we have more important things to do.

If you are stressing out over meditation because of this you have two options. Your first choice is to work on time management. Using time management you can actually schedule in your meditation sessions, so you feel perfectly fine sitting down and actually doing it. Time management can also help make it so you have fewer concerns as to what you can be doing instead, as you can use time management to get more things done.

Your second option is to simply work on letting things go. Sure the thoughts can be a bit distracting, okay they can be very distracting, but you need to work on letting these thoughts simply drift through your mind, don't make yourself aware of them. This is going to take some serious practice, but in time you will get better at not engaging in these thoughts and letting them simply pass you by.

Have To Practice A Lot Before You See Benefits

One thing you have to realize is that a lot of the research on meditation shows that long term meditation provides the best results. In fact, research shows that the more you meditate the better, regular sessions led to lower stress levels, a healthier and happier life, and you will find that you get more and more out of each session the longer you practice. So, while this might sound great, it can be a bit discouraging for people in the beginning, as they feel that they aren't seeing any kind of benefit from their first few sessions.

If this is you what you need to do is take notice of the research that has been done on the short term benefits of meditation. There is plenty of research out there that suggests just after six weeks of regular meditation sessions you will be more resilient to stress. It has also been shown that even just five minutes of meditation can have a positive effect on your body's reaction to stress.

With that being said don't give up, no matter how discouraged you might be. The worst thing that can happen is you get feeling down and then have no desire to continue on with your meditation sessions, which is only going to rob you of the numerous benefits.

Not Doing It Right

Out of all of the problems people face with meditation this has got to be the most popular one. Many people, including perfectionists, often wonder if they are doing meditation right. In fact, majority of these people often "know" that they are not doing it right. In thinking this they tend to give up before they even get started. What you need to realize is that yes meditation can be hard to master at first; some people find it harder than others though. Letting go of your thoughts is not quite as easy as it sounds, but getting discouraged and giving up is not going to help at all.

For people who are what we like to call achievement oriented sitting still and doing "nothing" can be quite difficult. Not only that but you are often used to be successfully at everything you do as soon as you try it, therefore having to practice something causes problems. If you have to work at mastering meditation you are probably having issues letting go of your thoughts because the trying is causing you to think more. Perfectionists face similar problems, as they don't want to do well; they want to do it perfectly every time. Having to do it perfectly can cause problems because you are judging yourself too harshly when you don't get it right the first time. For competitive people meditation can be hard because they are measuring up their performance to others, they simply want to be the best at meditation. And, meditation is not a sport or activity that one would consider competitive.

If any of the above scenarios sounds like something that you are dealing with there is help for you. You can still learn to master meditation, but you will need to make some changes. The most important change you will need to make is in relaxing your standards, don't expect yourself to be better than others and don't expect to do it perfectly each and every time. What you need to do is just focus on setting goals you can achieve, such as sitting still for five minutes and focusing on your breathing. Setting smaller goals that you can achieve will show you that you can be successful at meditation without discouraging yourself.

The other thing that you will need to change is accepting the fact that even people who have been meditating for years have troubles letting go of their thoughts some days. You need to come to terms with the fact that there is no perfect method of meditation. What works for one person might not work for you, so if you are having problems trying a different style of meditation can help.

Chapter 14:
Implementing Meditation into Everyday Life

Sometimes it's difficult to start a new habit, and it's especially harder to start one when we're already stressed out and feeling low about our life situation. However, there are some six easy ways to incorporate meditation into your daily life that's not invasive.

Practice Mindfulness

This is the core of meditation. Mindfulness is the practice of being aware of what you're doing exactly in the moment rather than thinking about the past or the future. You can take a moment to focus completely on your breathing in a moment of stress, or you can practice it at lunch or dinner as you're eating. No matter what you're doing, become specifically aware of how your body is feeling in that moment.

Follow a Healthy Lifestyle

I don't mean you have to change everything about your life right this instant, but start making small changes like eating a healthier breakfast or taking a salad for lunch. Make a point of exercising for a few minutes by getting up and going to the printer or the copier a few times a day if you work in an office. Try to make small changes that will lead to an overall large change of living a healthier lifestyle. Meditation is great for this because those who mindfully eat usually choose healthier food options, and those who visualize are more likely to complete their goals.

Read Spiritual Books

This method is not for everyone, but sometimes reading a sacred writing will help you understand meditation and help you strive for inner peace and understanding. If you choose not to read a spiritual book about religion, try one that's about the human element.

Participate in a Guided Meditation Class

Not only does this help you if you're unsure as to where you should begin, but it makes you form a commitment. You've signed up and paid for a class, so you're more likely to attend it. Sometimes this is best for beginners because it makes them more motivated.

Meditate at the Same Time

As aforementioned, meditation at the same time every day will help you form the habit of doing it daily. However, it's imperative that you meditate a few hours after you've eaten as it may interfere with your concentration if you experience gastrointestinal upset. In addition, most people choose to meditate in the morning because it's the most stress-free time of the day.

Understand the Journey

If you are able to comprehend that meditation is not just an exercise but a journey to your inner self and your subconscious, then you will be able to incorporate it better into your life. The entire purpose of meditation is to reach inner peace and a state of just being.

It is imperative that you know it can take years to reach a state of just being. If you feel calm and happy by the end of your meditation session, you have been successful. Don't become frustrated if you feel that you're not reaching that state of complete bliss because not everyone reaches it in their lifetime. It should be just enough that you are able to attain some form of inner peace through meditation.

Taking Advantage of 5-Minute Meditation

One thing that you will find yourself or others saying is they don't have enough time to practice meditation every day. Granted yes everybody has a schedule that they must follow, but that doesn't mean you can't make time each day to practice some kind of meditation.

Most things that you read in regards to meditation talk about how you need to spend around 10 minutes a day meditating, if not more. However, for some of us finding those ten extra minutes can be rather tough, so forget about finding anything longer than ten minutes. Now in some cases it comes down to prioritizing your needs, after all if you really want to do it you will figure out a time that works for you, but some days we simply just can't squeeze it in no matter how hard we try.

After reading this eBook you are well aware of just how beneficial mediation can be for you, whether it is physically, mentally, or even emotionally. So knowing how good meditation is for you, chances are you want to start practicing it right away and it is something that you want to engage in each day without fail. However, the problem is your crazy or perhaps even insane schedule. If you find it hard to set aside at least ten minutes every day, then 5 minute mediation is probably the best choice for you.

Here are the steps you will need to take when practicing 5 minute meditation, plus some tips to help things go smoothly.

Step One: Set A Timer

If you are limited on time setting a timer for 5 minutes is your best bet. Knowing you have a timer set will allow you to not worry about how long you have been meditating, which can distract you from the task at hand. For those of you with iPhones, consider using the Healing Music app as a timer.

Step Two: Relax

Now you need to sit down and relax, which can be done with your eyes closed or at least half way closed. If you don't want to close your eyes at least cast your glance down towards your lap to ensure you are focusing on what matters not on the scene around you. Breathing from your diaphragm take a few deep breaths and rid your body of all tension.

Step Three: Clear Your Mind

Now that you are relaxed you need to totally clear your mind of any kind of thoughts. Don't try thinking about nothing though as that will be counterproductive. Instead you need to focus on being. As thoughts enter your mind, as they will throughout the enter session, acknowledge each thought but let it go. The main goal is to continue refocusing yourself so that you are focusing on being in the moment at hand.

Step Four: Repeat

Simply continue with the breathing and focusing foe the entire 5 minutes. And what you will discover after those brief five minutes is that you feel more relaxed and refreshed than you did before you started meditating. If you do this every day you will notice even bigger differences in how less stressed you are.

Now that you know how to meditate in five minutes, you need to focus on doing it successfully. One of the first things you will need to figure out is a comfortable position, as well as comfortable clothes. If you are even the tiniest bit uncomfortable you are going to be distracted, which will be counterproductive to meditation.

You will also need to determine if you want to meditate in total silence or if you prefer some kind of music. Music, as long as it is the right kind, as well as aromatherapy can actually enhance your session. So if you are looking to change things up or get more out of your meditation try adding one or the other.

One mistake that many beginners make is they worry about whether or not they are doing it right. What you need to realize is that doing this actually makes things more stressful, which is counterproductive to what you are trying to achieve. Instead of focusing on your technique you are going to want to focus on keeping yourself in the present moment.

Meditation can be used for both short and long term purposes. Many people find these quick five minute sessions to be helpful when they need something to help quickly calm them down. However, the more frequently you practice meditation the easier time you will have coping with stress, you will be far less likely to react to various stresses in your life. And, while 5 minute sessions are great, you should also try and squeeze in longer sessions a few times a week.

Chapter 15:
Mindfulness Exercises For Everyday Life

Mindfulness is a great way to help relieve stress, but it also provides you with several other emotional and physical health benefits. One reason why it is such as great tool to adopt in your life is because of how fast it can bring about results, but also because it can be practiced any time.

We have already talked about mindfulness meditation earlier in this eBook, so we are not going to include that exercise in detail in this chapter. But we do want to encourage you to include it with these other mindfulness exercises in your everyday life.

With that being said let's take a quick look at other mindfulness exercises that you can adopt into your everyday life that are both convenient and simple.

Deep Breathing

In our chapter on breathing we go into detail about how to practice deep breathing, but here we want to talk about how it relates to mindfulness. Deep breathing allows you to experience mindfulness because you are focusing on the present moment. The best part about deep breathing is it can be done at any time, even as you are going about your day. With deep breathing you simply focus on your breathing, on both the sound and rhythm. You will quickly notice just how calm and relaxed you start to feel.

Music

We cannot stress enough about how important music is to meditation and just relaxing your mind and body in general. Music meditation is just one way that you can use music therapeutically. Listening music is a great way to practice mindfulness. When listening to music you can choose any kind of music that you like, but you want to avoid music that is fast-paced and has lyrics. A big part of the mindfulness exercise is to really listen to the music, feel each note as it plays. Focus on how the music makes you feel, what you are feeling right this minute as you listen to the song. Focus only on those thoughts, not any others that might enter your head.

Cleaning House

This mindfulness exercise actually has two meanings. The first part of this exercise is literal; you will seriously clean your house for this exercise. The other meaning is figurative and refers to the emotional baggage you will be getting rid of as you literally clean your house. The first step to using the literal meaning as a mindfulness exercise is to view it as a stress reliever rather than a chore. As you are cleaning focus on the task at hand, nothing else. Focus on how the cloth feels as you dust the entertainment center or how the vacuum vibrates in your hands as it moves across the floor. You can even add music to make it even more of a mindfulness exercise. As you focus on the task at hand, let go of all of your thoughts. Once you are done with the task it is amazing at how relaxed and rejuvenated you will feel.

Watch Your Thoughts

If you are like most people out there you have a constant stream of thoughts playing through your head. In fact it is all of this mind chatter that makes it hard for most of us to sit and focus on meditation; we simply don't know how to rein those thoughts in and are too afraid to try. Instead of letting your thoughts just run rampant through your mind, which can cause you more stress than you realize you might want to try watching your thoughts. To do this you simply need to sit back and watch your thoughts as they parade through your mind, don't try turning them off. Instead visualize each thought, in time you will find that they become quieter and you feel less stressed.

Observation

One of the most overlooked exercises in terms of mindfulness is the power of observation. To help practice mindfulness you need to pick an object that is lying around the room you are currently sitting in. It makes no difference what object you pick, so you can pick the first thing that you lay eyes on. Now pick this item up and hold it in your hands. Become absorbed in the object, but simply observe it, don't think about it or study it, just look at it for what it is. Interesting to note is you can do this same exercise by listening rather than looking. In fact, most people who practice mindful listening find it to be more powerful than observing.

One Minute Mindfulness

One of the benefits to this exercise is that it can be done anywhere at any time. In fact, you can try it right now as soon as you are done reading about it. The one minute mindfulness exercise involves setting a timer or a watch for exactly one minute. For that minute you are going to put all of your focus on your breathing. You don't need to close your eyes or do anything special, just sit back and breathe normally. As your mind wanders off, which it will do, redirect your focus back onto your breathing.

While this might seem like a silly exercise, it is a lot more powerful than you realize. Even people who have been meditating for years can struggle with an entire minute of alertness. Practicing every day will soon get you on the path of alertness and even better is the better you get the longer you can extend the duration of the exercise.

In case you haven't noticed one of the great things about mindfulness exercises is that they can be just about anything you choose. If none of these exercises catch your attention, simply go ahead and create your own. The important part is practicing every day so that you become less stressed over time. Mindfulness can also help you become more grounded.

Mindfulness Is Not Concentration

In order to fully understand mindfulness you need to realize that mindfulness is not the same thing as concentration, despite how similar they might seem. Now concentration is very important, as it is something that helps you focus your attention on whatever task is at hand. Concentration is what gives you command of your mind, it allows you to focus your mind and shut off the constant flow of thoughts. Mindfulness on the other hand is an awareness; it is about you being present in the moment at hand.

The distinction between the two can be hard to understand. So to gain a better idea of the difference between concentration and mindfulness let's talk a little bit about how to practice mindfulness. Understanding how to practice it can also help those of you who want to take advantage of the concept, but are having a hard time understanding how exactly.

Practicing Mindfulness

We have all heard or been told to start living in the moment, but being told to do so, doesn't help those of us who want to do so. Practicing mindfulness everyday is the best way to start living in the moment as it makes you aware of the present moment and of being in it.

The first thing you need to realize with mindfulness is that you don't have to concentrate really hard on it. All you need to do is become aware of the present moment. To do this take a brief moment and listen to the moment. Don't listen to the thoughts in your head; listen to the stuff around those thoughts, which is simply put awareness.

Now you might find this a bit hard to master, but there is no real magic formula that you can use to master mindfulness, it is something that just happens. Through exercises and activities you will learn to become aware of the present moment and will be able to live in the exact moment.

Using your breathing is one of the best ways to train yourself to become aware. Breathing is something that you do every day, all day and it is something that you can focus on anytime and anyplace.

With mindfulness you need to make a choice to become aware of your breathing. Follow the in and out movement of each breath with your mind, make sure you are feeling the movements of your stomach moving in and out and you inhale and exhale. Now you need to keep your awareness on your breathing, no matter what else happens. Realize that even though you are focused on your breathing you can still do other things; you can walk around or even participate in other tasks. Mindfulness doesn't mean you zone out or suppress all of your thoughts, it's just about focusing and feeling what is going on at the present moment.

Choose to be mindful over and over again. It might seem like a lot of work in the beginning, but over time it will be easier and become second nature.

Conclusion

Thank you again for downloading this book! I hope this book was able to help you learn how to feel better and change your state of mind in just a minute. The next step is to put the methods explained in the previous chapters into practice. As you read the chapters, there may have been one in particular that you think would work best for you. Then again, you may need to put all the methods into practice before you know what is most suitable.

Of course, there are many other ways that you can make yourself feel better. Some people may opt for a shopping trip or a spa day. Others may feel the need to talk things through with a trusted friend or loved one, or watch a favorite television program. Those are all viable ways of improving your state of mind. However, the disadvantage is that they are quick but fleeting fixes. They may work momentarily, but what happens the next time you feel down? You probably can't afford to go on a shopping trip every time a negative thought creeps into your mind.

Cognitive behavioral therapy, meditation and visualization can seem unattainable to some, particularly because they are not necessarily quick fixes; it may take several tries before you are finally able to put them into practice successfully. However, the reason that they are such important buzzwords is that many people have found that they work. Athletic coaches, for example, often train athletes to visualize their success before a race. Don't give up the first time you try one of those methods, and it doesn't work; leave it a day or so and try again. Once you have become more adept at following the instructions, you will be able to train yourself to improve your state of mind in just a minute.

Exercise is perhaps a more attainable method of changing your state of mind, but don't forget that you should fit it into your life anyway. Hopefully, that will improve your overall state of mind so that the negative thoughts you have are fewer and far between. Then when you do start to feel low, you can simply do a minute or so of your favorite exercise and hopefully, you will soon be back on track and feeling good about yourself.

The next step is to apply the steps and principles that are contained in this book into your life. Also, if you have friends or family members who badly need life transformation, share this book with them. It is my goal to help many people to achieve the life of their dreams.

Finally, if you enjoyed this book, then I'd like to ask you for a favor, would you be kind enough to leave a review for this book on Amazon? It'd be greatly appreciated!

Thank you and good luck!

Free Bonus 1

Morning Routine
to Wake Up Successful

Learn to Start your Day with Motivation and Energy to Upgrade Your Life Forever!

Table of Content

Introduction

Most people who don't already have a morning ritual get up at different times in the morning and they feel sluggish for hours after they're out of bed. That's one reason to start having a morning ritual, but did you know there are others?

A morning ritual actually gives you a reason to get out of your bed rather than lie in bed for half an hour as you stare at the ceiling or catch up on sleep. It also becomes a habit so that you get out of bed at a regular time. That will leave you feeling refreshed and awake all in and of itself. You'll also be starting the day off on the right foot rather than feeling sluggish and slow until well past lunchtime by doing some exercises and eating a healthy breakfast.

If you have a morning ritual, you will feel less rushed and you'll be more relaxed as you're getting ready and heading off to work or school. You'll be giving yourself the needed time to get your mindset right and your body awake. And most importantly, your morning ritual is all about you! You get to spend the needed amount of time every morning in order to center your mind and get your body healthy.

So let's get started with Chapter One: A Good Morning Starts with a Good Night.

Chapter One:
A Good Morning Starts with a Good Night

When people think of a good morning routine, they start by thinking about the moment they open their eyes to the sound of their alarm clock. In all reality, you cannot have a good morning routine without first having a good night's rest. So let's talk about a good nightly routine in order to get you into the habit of getting up when your alarm clock goes off the next morning.

Go to Bed When You're Tired and Wake-up at the Same Time Every Day

First and foremost, never go to bed unless you are actually tired. If you do this, you will mess up your internal clock and you'll never be able to get up on time in the morning. The second thing to do is to make sure you set your alarm clock at the same time every morning, including weekends. Your body will adjust within a matter of days; although, it will take thirty days before you can get up without the alarm clock. When your body has adjusted, it will tell you when it's time for bed at night.

Write down Three Things You're Proud Of

Before you go to bed, you should have a journal where you keep your affirmations for the morning and your good deeds from the day before. Write down three things that you did during the day that you're proud of such as coming up with a great idea at work or just holding the door for someone behind you. It doesn't matter how small the deed may seem, just write it down. Out of the worst day of your life, you will still be able to find three good things that happened. This will give you a positive mindset for the next morning.

Make Time for Family

If you have children, pick a specific time every night that you read them a bedtime story, and be sure to teach them good habits too, such as taking a bath at the same time, brushing their teeth at the same time, and having their bedtime story read to them at the same time. This creates a routine for both you and your children. In addition, be sure to ask them about their day and include them in your evening conversations in order for them to feel as if they're part of the family.

When it comes to your spouse, ask them about their day and talk about relaxing subjects. Avoid hot topics such as politics or religion, and don't bring up any arguments the two of you may have had. Leave those for another time.

Turn off Electronics

Serotonin is the neurotransmitter that prompts us to sleep, and when you have bright lights such as a cell phone or tablet screen directly in front of you as you're attempting to fall asleep, it will take a lot longer because the serotonin will not be released. Therefore, you should turn off all electronics sixty minutes before your planned bedtime. This will prompt you to fall asleep a lot quicker. In addition, turn all your lights down low rather than keeping bedtime lamps burning bright.

Set a Timer to Remind You to Sleep

Just like you set a timer to wake up, set one on your phone to tell you that it's time to shut your electronics off and to turn down your lights. This will help you keep a routine when you're going to bed.

Straighten Up

By putting items back in the place where they belong, you will feel much better about going to bed. Plus, you won't have to worry about doing that in the morning, which will leave you more time to get your morning routine packed full of energizing steps!

Prepare for Morning

If your kids' lunches can be prepared the night before, then do it. If you can set up your breakfast the night before, then get it prepared. There are a lot of things you can do the night before in order to set-up for your routine in the morning.

Practice Mindfulness

There's one simple way to make your mind relax, and that's to relax your body, too. Try a simple mindfulness meditation trick known as the body scan. To do this, you simply lie down in bed on your back. Then tense your right foot and release it. Do the same with your left, and continue up your body until you've tensed your face and relaxed. You should feel the blood flowing through your limbs and your mind should be focused on how relaxed you feel.

Take a Warm Bath

Taking a warm bath was something you did at night in order to get ready for bed when you were a child, but you can do it as an adult too. You don't have to wash your hair if you're going to shower in the morning, but you can submerge your body in the warm water and think about some of the positive things that happened to you that day. Brush your teeth when you get out so that you have a clean feeling when you wake up in the morning.

Drink a Glass of Warm Milk or Herbal Tea

Warm milk has the same amino acid in it known as tryptophan that turkey does, and it's the reason everyone is sleepy after a turkey dinner. Warming up a mug of milk in the microwave for thirty seconds and sipping it will make you feel sleepy within fifteen minutes. It's also a great way to hydrate yourself before bedtime so that you don't wake up thirsty in the middle of the night if it's wintertime.

In addition to milk, herbal, decaffeinated teas are a great way to stay hydrated and they cut out the craving for a cup of coffee or a glass of soda before bed, both of which are caffeinated. Caffeine is one of the main reasons most people are not able to get to sleep at night. In fact, cut off your caffeine consumption by three in the afternoon in order to be caffeine free by the time you want to go to bed.

Chapter Two:
Moving Around Wakes You Up

Getting up and going for a run in the morning before we've even had our first cup of coffee is not everyone's idea of a great morning exercise. In fact, you shouldn't be doing anything too strenuous until you've had time to stretch your muscles and release those amino acids from the various parts of your body to get you energized and feeling lithe. But first, let's get you some motivation to start doing morning exercises.

Here are nine interesting facts that will, hopefully, entice you to add exercise to your morning routine.

- Ninety percent of those who exercise in the morning exercise consistently.

- Those who exercise in the morning jumpstart their metabolism and sometimes it stays elevated for twenty-four hours.

- You'll feel more energized for the day and be able to think quicker than someone who hasn't exercised in the morning.

- Exercising in the morning will put you into a healthy mindset and you won't find yourself overeating or eating unhealthy foods at lunch and dinner.

- By exercising in the morning, you will actually regulate your circadian and endocrine rhythms and this will lead you to getting a better night's sleep and waking up more refreshed in the morning.

- o When your endocrine and circadian rhythms actually have a rhythm, it's much easier to wake up when your alarm clocks goes off in the morning.

- o You feel more alert in the morning when you wake up because your endocrine system is awake before you are.

- Many find that it's a good time to think about the rest of their day and plan ahead.

- People who exercise in the morning increase their mental acuity, and it can last anywhere from four to ten hours after exercise.

- Exercising in the morning is the best for your schedule because it ensures that nothing else will take precedence over it.

- People who exercise on a regular basis have a high quality of sleep and actually require less sleep every night.

Now that you have some incentive, which exercises are best to do in the morning if you're just beginning to exercise? And which exercise burn more calories and leave you feeling more alert? Well, here's a chart to let you know how many calories you can burn if you're interested in losing weight, and then I'll give you an example exercise routine that involves stretching, minor cardio, and some weight lifting if you're feeling particularly adventurous.

Exercise Type	Calories Burned	Amount of Time
Running/Jogging (5 MPH)	295	30 Minutes
Bicycling (10 MPH)	195	30 Minutes
Swimming	255	30 Minutes
Aerobics	240	30 Minutes
Basketball	220	30 Minutes
Walking (3.5 MPH)	140	30 Minutes
Weight Training	110	30 Minutes
Stretching	90	30 Minutes
Biking	145	30 Minutes
Dancing	165	30 Minutes

So now that you know how many calories you're burning, let's take a look at a beginner's routine, and then we'll add in some more strenuous exercises for those who already exercise during the day but want to add a routine to their morning schedule.

For Beginners

For those who are looking for exercises that will help them wake up and get their blood flowing, but won't make them feel as if they've run a marathon, these are some excellent exercise choices.

Back Stretch

This is actually a yoga exercise that will help you strengthen your back as well as get your digestive system moving. Simply lie on your back on the floor or a yoga mat and hug both your knees to your chest. Then raise your head and shoulders off the floor and hold this position for fifteen seconds, breathing deeply by raising your abdomen up and down rather than using your chest. Then release slowly and repeat this exercise ten times with ten second breaks in between, and do four repetitions.

Cat-Cow Position

It sounds a bit odd, but the cat-cow movement will help strengthen your core, as well as stretch out your back muscles and your abdominal muscles. Start by lying down on your stomach and bring yourself up into a kneeling position with your hands on the floor in front of you. Then inhale and tuck your tailbone as you round your back and look toward your belly button. Then exhale and drop your belly as you arch your lower back and look up.

Do this ten times and repeat the sets of ten four times.

Shoulder Stretch

This is an excellent way to get yourself motivated just as you get out of bed, or a good way to cool down after a long workout. Simply reach your right hand back over your should and reach your left hand back behind you. Then clasp your hands together and hold this position for ten to fifteen seconds. Then switch to your left hand over your shoulder and your right hand behind your back and hold again. Repeat this four times.

Intermediate Positions

If you're looking to build some muscle and lose a little weight, as well as tone your body, then these exercises should help. Keep in mind that doing a few stretches before you begin these is a good idea as they can be strenuous when you first start out.

Prisoner Squat

To perform the prisoner squat, stand with your feet shoulder width apart and be sure that your posture is correct. Then put your hands behind your head as if you're being arrested, and lower your body with your hips back and bend your knees. Go down as far as you can. Pause for a few seconds, and then slowly push back up to the starting position. Do this four times with one minute breaks in between and ten repetitions.

The High Kneed Walk

Stand with your feet shoulder width apart and make sure your back is straight. Then, without changing how you're standing, raise your left knee as high as possible and step forward. Do not round your lower back. Repeat with your right leg and do this for thirty seconds.

The Mount Climber

Get on your hands and knees and then assume the pushup position with your arms straight. Lift your right leg off the floor and bring it as close to your chest as you can. Then touch the floor with your right foot. Go back to the starting position and repeat with your left leg. Then alternate back and forth for thirty seconds. Do ten repetitions.

Experienced

Once you've moved past working out with just your own body weight, you've moved into the experienced category. Now, in order to get yourself into shape, you must use hands weights or dumbbells. Try starting out with just one pound dumbbells and moving up incrementally as you become comfortable.

The Dumbbell Squat

This is exactly like the intermediate squat except you're adding weights. Hold the weights in your hands and assume the position with your feet placed shoulder width apart and tighten your abdominal muscles as you stand straight. Then lower your body as far as you can and pause. Rise back up slowly and repeat ten times.

The Row

This is definitely one that can become difficult if you're a beginner, so be aware of how far to push your body and don't go too crazy with this one. Hold your dumbbells in your hands and stand up straight. Then lower yourself as if you're sitting in a chair and hold that position. Your arms should be loose and your palms should be facing behind you. Then bring the dumbbells up to the side of your torso and pause. Slowly lower them back. Repeat this ten times.

Chapter Three:
Affirmations during Hygienic Routine

After waking up and doing your exercises, taking a shower is probably in order. But did you know that you can kill two birds with one stone? While you're taking a relaxing shower, why not repeat some of your daily affirmations to yourself? Let's take a look at why so many people are starting to repeat affirmations and how you can come up with a few on your own.

What is an affirmation, and why should I use them?

Affirmations are a series of words that usually form a sentence saying something about yourself or something you want to happen, and they're aimed at affecting your conscious and your subconscious mind. At this point, you might be asking if this is brainwashing yourself. In fact, it's a little like that, except these are positive things that will eventually become a reality for you because everything you do throughout the day is aiming at making those affirmations come true.

What do they do?

Affirmations should be motivating in order to get you to do the tasks you need to accomplish in order to complete your goal. Therefore, an affirmation should be aimed at keeping you on track. If you're using them properly, they will activate the subconscious mind and the powers that are within your mind lying dormant.

An affirmation will ultimately change the way you think, the way you behave, and bring you into contact with new people and new goals. They should make you feel positive and energized when you're finished saying them.

When should I say them and how many times?

You can say them at any time during the day, but the best times to say them are before you go to bed and during your morning routine. You can choose to say them during your hygiene routine or you can choose to say them as you're visualizing or meditating, or even when you first wake up in order to get yourself motivated to get out of bed. You may even choose to repeat them as many times as you wish throughout the day.

Before you begin, though, you should ask whether or not you actually want what you're going to ask for. If there's any doubt that you want what you're asking for, you will stand in the way of yourself. Therefore, be sure you want that job promotion before you begin.

Use love, faith, feeling, and interest when you are affirming. Talk as if you have already fulfilled the affirmation rather than saying that it *will* happen. By doing this, you are accelerating the fulfillment of the affirmation.

What are some examples of affirmations?

You can choose to use these affirmations specifically if they really speak to you, but really you ought to change them to suit your needs. By making them personal, you are making them resonate more with your subconscious.

- For Success

    - I can achieve success because it is simple and easy.

    - Success is always seeking me.

    - I can feel success flowing into my life.

    - I am achieving my goals.

    - Every time I inhale, I am filling with prosperity, and every time I exhale, I am ridding myself of failure.

- Happiness

    - Happiness is manifesting in my life right now.

    - I deserve to be happy and will be happy.

    - Happiness is seeking me.

    - I am breathing in happiness and breathing out depression.

    - I am happy right now.

- Health

    - I am functioning perfectly and all my systems are happy.

    - Healing energy is filling me right now.

    - I can feel the universe filling me with healing energy.

- Each cell of my body is filled with healing energy and singing with happiness.

- My health is improving day by day.

- Money

  - Money is flowing into my life freely.

  - I am obtaining more and more money daily.

  - I am a money magnet.

  - The universe is sending more money my way daily.

  - I am earning a lot of money.

- Self-Confidence

  - I am beautiful.

  - I am worthy of being loved.

  - Many people love me.

  - The universe is sending a lot of love my way.

  - I am important.

Notice how each of these affirmations focuses on the person as an individual and is specific about their concerns. Repeat these to yourself out loud as you're doing your hair or makeup in the mirror, or do them mentally as you're brushing your teeth. You'll feel clean inside and out when you're doing your affirmations as you're doing your daily hygiene routine.

Chapter Four:
Eating a Healthy Breakfast

You've heard the saying that breakfast is the most important meal of the day, but do you know why? Most of us took it upon good faith because our mothers told us to eat breakfast because it would help us grow up strong and healthy, and they weren't wrong. Breakfast is the most important meal of the day because it is the meal that breaks your fast from food overnight, which brings your body out of ketosis. Ketosis is the state in which our bodies burn fat rather than calories we're eating, and what better way to break that fast than to put something really healthy into our systems?

Eating a healthy breakfast is linked to weight control, better performance throughout the day, strength and endurance during physical activities, and lower cholesterol levels. That translates to a healthier, better you. So don't skip the morning meal and make it a good one!

Here are some tips on how to make your breakfasts healthier.

Add Protein

Did you know that protein is an essential building block of the body's cells? It's also the best food to help blunt hunger because ultimately our bodies are craving protein and not much else. When we eat enough protein, our minds immediately tell our bodies we're no longer hungry.

The traditional breakfast of eggs is actually one of the best things you can eat. Those commercials and the food companies are not lying to you, for once. They're telling the truth when eggs are packed full of vitamins and protein. If that's not convincing enough, one study conducted by Pennington Biomedical Research Center had two groups, overweight women who ate bagels for breakfast and overweight women who ate eggs for breakfast. The calories between the eggs and the bagel were actually the same amount, yet the women who ate eggs lost sixty-five percent more weight.

In addition to being great for weight loss, eggs actually make you feel fuller quicker and longer. Therefore, you spend less time agonizing what you're going to be eating for lunch and more time working on that project you know you have to get done. So if you don't have any serious heart problems or cholesterol issues eat two eggs for breakfast and even add a slice of bacon.

The Truth about Cereal

I'm not talking about Captain Crunch or Cocoa Puffs. They're okay as a snack occasionally, but you should really be eating some healthy, whole grain cereals, and they should have no added sugar, too. A Harvard study of over 17,000 men determined that men who ate breakfast cereal frequently weighed less than those who didn't eat breakfast cereal.

As long as it's a healthy cereal and a reasonable amount, breakfast cereal will actually make you feel full and energized throughout the morning.

So What about Other Foods?

I'm glad you asked. There are so many different foods you can eat for breakfast that are healthful and beneficial to your body! This is just a short list of common foods that you can try out for breakfast. Find a few favorites and get started having a healthy, energizing breakfast tomorrow morning.

- Some whole-wheat toast with a vegetable omelet.

- A homemade breakfast sandwich consisting of a whole-wheat English muffin, cheese, a scrambled egg, and a slice of tomato or maybe ham.

- A smoothie with yogurt and fruit.

- A whole-grain bagel with cream cheese and a slice of smoked salmon.

- Some whole-grain cereal with fruit and milk.

- A glass of orange juice and some oatmeal with raisins and nuts.

- Some fruit in low-fat yogurt.

- A breakfast bar.

- A banana and a hard-boiled egg.

- Half a grapefruit.

- A slice of whole-wheat bread with almond butter.

- A cup of blueberries.

Pretty much any type of fruit is healthy to eat for breakfast, and something that has protein such as yogurt, peanut butter, almond butter, Nutella, any meat or eggs. The list is almost endless to what you can eat for breakfast every morning.

A quick note; some people prefer to eat a light breakfast before they start working out. There aren't any benefits to eating breakfast before or directly after a workout, so it's really a personal preference. However, your body is going to need protein in order to replenish the muscles you just broke down, so keep that in mind the next time you're heading for a donut. Those aches in your arms and legs will go away much quicker with an egg than a pastry.

Chapter Five :
Visualization before Starting the Day and Meditation for Stress Relief

Meditation and visualization are not interchangeable. They are two vague concepts that have to be narrowed down to your specific values and basically how your mind works on a subconscious level. For example, one person might need movement during meditation while another might need absolute stillness. In this chapter, I'm going to touch on some basic visualization and meditation techniques, but don't be afraid to look outside of this source for other types in order to find one that works best for you.

First, let's talk about what meditation is and why you should be doing it. Meditation is basically a state of deep concentration where your mind is being given one point of focus rather than bouncing around from one topic to the next. A lot of people give up on this practice because they are constantly thinking about other things as they're meditating, but it takes practice and concentration on the body rather than the mind to succeed. But once you do, you'll wonder why it took you so long to try this in the first place!

Now, let's discuss visualization. Visualization is actually a form of meditation, but you're focusing on an image. There are two different forms, visual or kinesthetic. A kinesthetic visualization is creating the experience of actually doing something within your mind. You will *feel* yourself going through that action using all five of your senses. This might be an image of you obtaining a job promotion or just something as simple as having a wonderful day. The other type of visualization, visual, is picturing a sequence of events or another person, but you're not really feeling it. The best type of visualization is both visual and kinesthetic.

There are forms of meditation that combine with visualization, but there are meditation techniques that do not involve visualization at all. In fact, they shy away from picturing any type of image because this is considered a thought. So let's discuss both techniques separately in great detail so that you fully understand what you are doing.

Visualization

Visualization is used to either relieve stress or bring about subconscious actions that will get you to where you want to go. For example, visualization that is for relaxation might include a picture of a calming place or a place that feels safe for you, such as a calming landscape or a deserted beach. Visualization can be used for healing, such as visualizing that the heart is working calmly and healthily. It can be used for performing an action perfectly such as scoring a goal in a soccer game. It can be used for mapping out what you're going to do and say during a business meeting in order to obtain a client or impress the boss.

When you're using visualization in meditation, your mind is concentrating as your physical body is relaxing. So in order to practice it, you should be sitting down in a comfortable position or even lying down, and you should be picturing and feeling what you're going to do that day. Leave all negative aspects out of your visual in order to bring about positives during the day.

You can also do this at night before you go to bed. It's an excellent technique to use when you're visualizing all the positive things you did that day and all the positive things you're going to do in the morning. While you're doing this, you should be breathing in an out evenly in order to remain in a calm, relaxed state.

Here's a step by step guide to get you started.

- Clear your mind and concentrate on your breathing.

- Create or imagine your visual image or feeling before you start this exercise, and then bring it up and relive it repeatedly as you're breathing.

- As you inhale, imagine your body is expanding with potential and as you exhale your positive thoughts are being expelled into the world. They're planting their seeds in order for you to have a successful day.

Meditation

Meditation, also known as mindfulness, is a mental practice that involves concentration and mantras or focusing on the breaths. It's particularly helpful for those who are under a lot of stress or can't seem to calm their minds enough to do their daily routine. Some choose to practice meditation as soon as they get out of bed while others choose to practice this technique just before they go off to work to start the day.

Here are some things to remember as you're meditating.

- Don't force it. Once you've obtained concentration, don't judge the thoughts or observations within your mind as either good or bad. Just let them flow by with a brief acknowledgment.

- Pay attention to what's happening inside your mind. You will notice things happening outside of your person such as sounds, sights, and feelings but don't allow those to distract you. Instead, focus on what's happening within your mind.

- Keep it up. Sometimes it takes a little while for your mind to adjust to this process. It might seem alien to you at first and frustrating, but don't give up. Give it at least thirty days in order to see if it's something that you can build into a habit.

- Redirect your thoughts. Sometimes they might wander to planning, daydreaming or even criticism of what you're doing, but redirect your mind to the present and what you should be visualizing.

Now with those thoughts in mind, let's take a look at some common mindfulness meditation techniques that you can start using in the morning.

Basic Meditation

This is something that all beginners should start with as it's very simple and uses a focal point that is easy to concentrate on.

1. Find a comfortable position in a chair or sit cross-legged on the floor.

2. Place your right hand on your abdomen and your left hand on your chest. Now breathe through your nostrils and count to four as you're doing so. You should be using your abdomen to breathe in and your chest should not be moving much. Then hold that breath for

seven seconds. Now exhale through your mouth for eight seconds.

3. Once you've fully concentrated on your breathing, you can let some of the outside inside. Listen to the sounds, sensations, and the ideas within you.

4. Remember not to judge any thoughts that come into your mind. Simply acknowledge them and allow them to pass.

5. If you find your mind is skipping from one topic to another, focus on your breathing again and start over.

Informal Meditation

Sometimes you need to start off with an introductory period before you start going directly into mindfulness meditation. It's reasonable to start off with only twenty minutes in the morning rather than going the entire forty-five minute length most professionals or experienced meditators do. It takes about twenty minutes for the mind to begin to calm; therefore, you should experience a calming feeling just before you're finished. Try some of these techniques to begin with if you're not comfortable with the previously mentioned method.

- Start by trying to practice while you're eating, showering, walking, or playing with your children.

- Concentrate on the sensations in your body and what you're currently sensing with all five senses.

- Breathe in through your nose and let your abdomen expand fully.

- Then breathe out through your mouth.

- Note how you feel as you inhale and exhale.

- Keep doing the task you were doing before but do it with full deliberation.

- Engage each sense (sight, sound, touch, taste, and smell) so that you can recall them later.

Conclusion

Thank you for reading The Morning Ritual! Hopefully, you've learned how to get your morning started off right by implementing a nightly routine, waking up on time at the same time every morning, starting to exercise, using affirmations, eating healthy, and practicing meditation. Let's take a look at an example routine in order to get you started on the right path.

1. Wake up at 6AM.
2. Stretch for fifteen minutes.
3. Workout for thirty minutes.
4. Say ten affirmations while showering.
5. Eating breakfast and repeat five more affirmations.
6. Meditate for half an hour.
7. Visualize my day for fifteen minutes before heading off to work.

You can change around the routine to fit your needs and your preferences, but be sure to include the exercise, a healthy breakfast, meditation, and affirmations in order to get your day started off right. Remember that a morning routine is not just to get you out the door on time; it's about making you feel positive, healthy, and ready for the rest of your day. And don't forget to create a nighttime ritual in order to wake up feeling refreshed in the morning already.

If you liked this book, please take the time to log onto the retailer you bought it from and leave a positive review!

Thank you and have a good morning!

www.ingramcontent.com/pod-product-compliance
Lightning Source LLC
Chambersburg PA
CBHW070301190526
45169CB00001B/496